OSWALD JACOBY ON

Poker

OSWALD JACOBY

ON

Poker

WITH A FOREWORD BY

GRANTLAND RICE

AND AN INTRODUCTION BY

WILLIAM E. McKENNEY

Doubleday, Doran & Company, Inc.

GARDEN CITY   1944   NEW YORK

PRINTED AT THE *Country Life Press*, GARDEN CITY, N. Y., U. S. A.

Acknowledgment

I wish to acknowledge the assistance given to me in the preparation of this book by Albert H. Morehead, Edward Hymes, Jr, Samuel Fry, Jr, Van H. Cartmell and James W. Poling.

OSWALD JACOBY

Foreword

No ONE has to spread the news abroad that Oswald Jacoby is one of the top bridge players in the history of the game. He has stood out for seven years in the national championship and other tournaments. Mr Jacoby is just as good at poker and just as keenly interested. He has played in every part of the country with every type of poker player and so is thoroughly qualified to write an authoritative book on this game. Poker is one of the oldest and most popular of all American card games. It has more interesting angles than almost any other game ever invented. Mr Jacoby has made this book not only informative and authoritative but extremely interesting, which is always the combination to be desired. This may well be the *last* word on poker.

GRANTLAND RICE

Contents

Introduction

I HAVE READ with interest the manuscript of Mr Jacoby's book on poker. In particular, since laws of card games have always been a hobby of mine, that part of the book appealed to me. A card game must have laws; someone must make them, and certainly Oswald Jacoby is the one person most properly qualified to do so for the game of poker.

For some time past I have consulted him whenever a difficult question on poker laws was presented to me. I am delighted that he has finally compiled a complete authoritative code.

WILLIAM E. McKENNEY

Chairman, National Laws Commission.
National Executive Secretary, American
Contract Bridge League.

OSWALD JACOBY ON
Poker

CHAPTER I

Poker—America's Own Card Game

THERE IS a popular misconception that since poker is a gambling game it is pure luck. Actually nothing could be further from the fact. Poker is the one game where a player may hold bad cards all evening and still come out a winner.

Poker is a game of money management—not card management. It is a game where there is a right technical play in every situation, and the winning player should know this correct technical play. But the winning player must go further. He must deliberately make the wrong technical play on a sufficient number of occasions so that the other players in the game will never be certain as to what he is doing. It is a game where conservatism pays. No poker player, however good, can afford to bet even a few chips in the early rounds when the possibilities presented by his hand are infinitesimal. At the same time no really good poker player can afford to play too "tight," because once a tight player bets, anyone who does not have a very good hand automatically drops out and the tight player never gets a chance to win the really big pots.

It is a game where the best hand need not win. It may be bluffed out. The good poker player must bluff on occasion. The man who never bluffs never wins since, like the tight player, no one ever calls him.

This fine American game has always been popular among men. In late years women have taken it up also, and today it is played almost as much, if not as much, as bridge; and all this popularity in spite of the fact that the game operates under local rules which are varied from time to time as new situations arise.

True, there are so-called laws of poker, but these are antiquated and in no sense cover the modern streamlined game.

It is my purpose in this book—

FIRST: to present a code of laws which will fully and simply cover the game as played today.

SECOND: to describe the variations which I believe are most enjoyable.

THIRD: to show how enjoyment can be obtained from poker without the necessity of heavy gambling.

FOURTH AND LAST: to show how to play poker.

CHAPTER II

How to Conduct a Poker Game

As long as people gamble there will be both losers and winners; and whatever the game—be it bingo, bridge or poker—and whatever the stakes, some of the losers will be losing more than they really can afford. In the old days this was particularly true of poker, which is one reason why, until recently, the game was held in considerable disrepute. Old-fashioned poker—i.e., straight Stud and Draw—were essentially tough games in which the only amusement was obtained through the gambling element. Today the new games suggested in this book are of sufficient interest so that people can play them for nominal stakes. However, even though the stakes are nominal, people will still get hurt if certain rules aren't adhered to.

First there is the matter of stakes. In this connection our recommendation is to set the stake at as small a figure as you can without boring the players. And once the stake has been set, adhere to it rigidly. In particular it is inadvisable toward the close of a game to raise the limit or the ante. Remember, the stake you have set is always one the players can afford. When you raise the ante or the limit you are increasing the size of the game and someone may get hurt.

Second, set a quitting time. When play begins everyone is exactly even—there are no winners and no losers. The players should know when they want to stop and should set a time for this. Once this stopping time is set, it should be adhered to rigidly. In particular the habit of playing even an extra half-hour should be discouraged.

Let us consider a typical mixed poker game. Two or three married couples and perhaps a couple of bachelors get together to play one or two evenings a week. Everyone has to get up the next morning, and accordingly twelve-thirty is fixed as the stopping time. As long as they adhere to this time rigidly, there is no harm done. True, the players may be the least bit tired the next morning, but they are not so tired as to interfere with their efficiency.

However, suppose they once play overtime, even half an hour. Let us see what happens. The next time they play some loser is sure to say at twelve-thirty: "You know last time we played till one. We ought to do it again tonight." No one can make any sound objection now, and instead of being a twelve-thirty game it has become a one-o'clock game.

This extra half-hour doesn't seem like much but it does represent trouble, because pretty soon we will find the game stopping at one-thirty, then at two, then at three, and finally we will have an all-night session, with the men rushing home at seven in the morning to shave and get to the office in no condition to be of any value to themselves or anyone else.

The next time the game is played everyone will resolve to quit early. They probably will—at, say, five o'clock, but not much before. The game, which has previously been a relaxation, becomes a serious event. One couple probably decides they won't play any more, and after a while it becomes impossible to get up any game whatsoever.

All the above assumes that the stakes remain the same even though play continues all night. Actually, once overtime play starts, there is a great tendency to raise the stakes. For instance, at twelve-thirty it is decided to play another hour. A player who is out one hundred chips says, "Let's double the limit for the extra hour. I want a chance to get even." The other players acquiesce. As a result, at one-thirty, which is the second quitting time, a man who was a big winner at half-past twelve is now a big loser. He says, "You ought to give me a chance. Let's play one more hour and double the limit again."

When the game finally breaks up at seven in the morning it is disclosed that the big loser is now out over a thousand chips, to say nothing of a night's sleep. If the chips have a value of a penny, that means ten dollars instead of one dollar; if the chips have a value of a dime, it means one hundred dollars instead of ten—in either case undoubtedly more than the evening's entertainment could possibly be worth to him.

A third point, which may sound a little sordid, is just as essential as the other two. That is, immediate settlement of every game. I know of one game which has run every afternoon except Sundays for twenty years. The game is played for fairly substantial stakes which, however, are well within the means of the players. Before they leave the table the losers pay what they owe either by cash or check, and the winners collect immediately. There is no bookkeeping from day to day except when a winner has gone home early, and even then there is no real bookkeeping. All that happens is that when he arrives the next day he receives his money, which has already been left for him the evening before. This is the only really satisfactory method of settling a game. When a person is allowed to get up from the table owing money, irrespective of the amount and irrespective of who the person who owes the money happens to be, trouble is bound to start. Let me just give an example:

A group of people are accustomed to play poker every Thursday night. On one particular Thursday Mr G loses to Mr A and says, "I haven't got a check with me. I'll pay you next Thursday." Next Thursday Mr G is out of town and A loses to B. A now says, "I haven't been paid from last Thursday's game. I'll pay you when G pays me."

The following week G appears but A is ill. B says to G, "You owe A from two weeks ago, and

A didn't pay me last week." G replies, "I'm awfully sorry about that but I sent A my check on Monday."

B now loses and fails to pay C. The first thing you know, everybody owes everybody else, the accounts get all balled up and the game breaks up in a row. And that applies to a case where the players are able to pay. Let us suppose in another game Mr X, one of the players, is hard up. He loses and says, "I'll pay next time." The next time comes and he loses again and makes another excuse that he will pay the following week. The following week he loses for the third time and now says, "I just can't pay. I've lost more than I can afford. I'll send you money when I can."

He drops out of the game, but the other players have been stuck for what he has lost in three sessions.

When you are accustomed to settle at the end of the game, however, the worst Mr X can do is to fail to pay after one session. Then, since he has not paid at the end of one session, he is automatically barred from the next session.

In order to make a poker game interesting it is a good idea to have a lot of chips in play at all times. In other words, a game where the limit is one hundred chips worth a penny each is much more fun than a game where the limit is ten chips worth ten cents each. And incidentally, the game with one hundred penny chips, while theoretically the same size as the game with ten ten-cent chips, actually is substantially smaller, the reason being that a player is much more cautious about putting one hundred penny chips in the pot than he would be with ten ten-cent chips.

In my opinion it is inadvisable ever to play with chips nominally worth less than a penny. But for those to whom Penny Ante is still too high a game there is a simple way of covering this difficulty. Play with penny chips, but when you come to settle the game pay off at five or ten cents on the dollar.

A nice variation if you want to restrict the losses is to play so-called Poverty Poker. Suppose it is determined in advance that no one should lose more than a dollar. Each person takes a dollar's worth of chips at the start, and the limit is so arranged that this dollar's worth of chips should last a long time, even with tough luck. However, if a person does lose all his dollar's worth of chips he gets another dollar's worth free and continues to play without any additional cash liability. If he loses the second dollar's worth he has to stop. And if he wins he must make good both dollars before he can take a profit. At the end of the game, in case any player has lost more than a dollar's worth of chips, the winners are charged the excess difference.

Bookkeeping

Bookkeeping errors are all too frequent in many poker games and, when they occur, always lead to a certain amount of unpleasantness. The first class of bookkeeping errors is due to mistakes in counting chips. For instance, in giving out a stack the banker will give one or two chips too many or too few. These errors are of relative unimportance since the amount involved is very small. However, I have seen games where the error might run into several stacks. This usually occurs when there are not enough chips and, as a result, the players in the game buy back and forth from one another. Then the banker, who is busy playing the game, enters the transactions incorrectly, and at the end the books are way out of balance.

Theoretically, when a bookkeeping error occurs all players in the game should be equally responsible whether they win or lose. Actually, however, it is customary and I believe reasonably proper, in the event the bookkeeping error results in a profit, to credit the profit to the losers; while if the bookkeeping error results in a loss, it is charged against the winners.

However, the best thing is not to have bookkeeping errors, and this can be pretty well taken care of if the following rules are used:

FIRST: the bookkeeping unit will always be one stack, and under no circumstances should transactions involving a fraction of a stack go on the books.

SECOND: all transactions should be between a player and the banker—never between two players.

THIRD: transactions should be restricted to a minimum. This can usually be done by use of markers. These markers may consist of chips of a special color, mah-jongg counters or even matchsticks. The marker should have a value equal to one stack, and when a player enters the game he should be given one stack of real chips and several markers. Then, as he loses chips, he may trade in a marker for a stack of chips at any time without any bookkeeping being involved at all.

FOURTH: the banker should enter each player's name on a sheet of paper with several columns after the name. He writes the number of stacks given the player initially in the first column. If the player takes more stacks later, he writes the accumulation in the second column. The next chips sold put the player in the third column, etc.

FINALLY: in order to avoid argument when this method is used it is a good plan for the player to put his initials in the column opposite the number of chips he has received so that there will be no question at the end of the game.

This last system of bookkeeping may arouse resentment. I can just hear someone say, "What sort of game is it where the banker cannot be trusted to write down how many chips he gives the various players?" The answer to that is that, irrespective of how honest and ethical people are, they can and do make mistakes. In particular I have heard more withering arguments between people of the highest probity as to whether or not John Smith has taken eight stacks or seven stacks than I care to remember. But when Smith has to sign for the stacks he receives there are no arguments at all and everybody is happy.

CHAPTER III

How to Conduct Yourself in a Poker Game

Lying, Bluffing, etc.

SINCE POKER by its very nature is a game of wile and artifice, in theory a player has the right to attempt to conceal his hand or mislead his opponent in any manner he desires. For instance, with a particularly good hand it is his privilege to hesitate, worry and fret before betting. He may look disgusted when he is really delighted with what is going on, or he may act very cheerful when he really knows that he is in great danger. He may make a large bet and say, "Boys, I sure have a hand this time!" when he is really bluffing, or in fact he may make practically any lying statement he desires.

While there are no rules on the subject, however, it is the privilege of those who wish to play poker to establish their own rules of conduct. Particularly there is one lying statement which I do not believe should ever be made. That is the statement by a player, "I am betting blind," meaning that he has not seen his hand or draw in Draw Poker or his hole card in Stud. Custom should definitely decree that a player making this statement must be telling the truth.

Although many people differ with me on this point, my own experience has been that a player who attempts to fool his opponents by means of gestures, actions, etc. is much easier to play against than one who makes all his bets and plays in the same manner. Accordingly I try to play as much in the manner of a wooden Indian as possible.

Acting Out of Turn

The worst possible offense against the proprieties of poker occurs when a player acts before his turn. Such action, even though it does the player himself no good, may vitally affect the rights of other players. The rules provide penalties for acting out of turn, but since these penalties are exceptionally moderate it is doubly important from the standpoint of ethics that players avoid this bad habit.

For instance, here is an extreme situation in Draw Poker: A opens the pot; B and C stay. After the draw A checks and B bets. Whereupon A immediately throws in his hand or indicates in some manner that he is not going to call. The effect of this pass, of course, is to help C to the detriment of B. For instance, C may decide that B is bluffing and call; whereas if A had not passed out of turn, C might not call on account of fear of what A would do. Or C might have a very good hand. With A still in the pot C might merely call, hoping to coax A in. With A out of the pot C will surely raise.

Let's take the same situation and suppose that A calls as soon as B bets. This call is likely to keep C from calling. Now if B is bluffing, he is not hurt since he loses the pot anyway, but if B really has a good hand, A's call out of turn has cost him the chips C might have put in.

Conversely a player should endeavor to know when it is his turn to bet and should act promptly. And of course it is unethical to sit back and try to coax someone to act out of turn so that you may obtain an advantage by seeing what he intended to do.

If a player wishes he may make gestures when it is not his turn to bet. For example, in a Table Stakes game Player A makes a bet; Player B is now considering what to do and looks over and sees that Player C is engaged in piling up a large number of chips with apparent intention of putting them all in the pot. Player B now drops, whereupon Player C simply calls, which is all he had intended doing in the first place. This trick will work occasionally but it comes under the head of mannerisms, and after a while your opponents will cease to be scared of you when you look threatening and really fear you when you take no apparent interest in what is going on.

Looking at Turned Cards

In Stud Poker knowledge of what cards have been turned down becomes important in deciding on the possibilities of your own and other players' hands. When a player turns down his cards out of turn, of course the other players have a right to ask to see the cards so turned down; but when a player folds in proper turn no one has a right to see his hand again, although it is customary in most games to show such cards to any player who asks to see them before betting. However, the player who asks should remember that he is being extended a courtesy and should not abuse this courtesy by asking on practically every hand.

Stacking Chips

In a Table Stakes game the players have the right to know how many chips the other players have. Therefore it is the duty of the players to keep their chips stacked neatly so that the other players can tell how many they have by observation. Failure to do this is simply minor sharking.

Rabbit Hunting

This consists of looking ahead in the deck to see what would have happened if you had stayed in the pot. If done after the hand is over, the rabbit hunter merely slows up the game and annoys the other players. If done while the hand is in progress, however, it is absolutely inexcusable since it not only definitely tends to upset the players remaining in the pot but furthermore the rabbit hunter frequently, in some manner or another, gives away what cards are coming next. While there is no penalty in the rules for this last offense, a great many games could be improved by means of a local rule to the effect that any player who looks at any undealt card before the completion of the hand should be compelled to immediately pay five chips into the pot. I guarantee this will cure anyone of the habit.

Looking at Another Hand

While a player who has dropped out of the pot has no right to look at another player's hand, in all except tough gambling games it is done. However, a player who looks at another's hand should realize that he is being rendered a definite courtesy and accordingly should do nothing to jeopardize the rights of the player at whose hand he may be looking. It is particularly bad form to look first at one hand and then at another since there is a definite impression conveyed that the first hand is not very strong, else you would be satisfied with looking at it and no other.

Sure Things

The whole purpose of poker is to get into a position where you do have a sure thing and then use that sure thing to collect as much from your opponent or opponents as possible. In spite of this obvious fact I recall numerous times I have been asked whether it is permissible to bet with a royal flush, etc. The answer is, of course it is all right. You will be betting on a sure thing, but remember, when you bet with a sure thing your opponent is by no means compelled to call you. When you check with a sure thing your opponent does not have to bet into it.

While this does not come under the head of how to conduct a poker game, I cannot go by this point without telling one of the many stories about the Thanatopsis Literary and Inside Straight Club which used to meet every Friday for an all-night poker session. Most of the members were and still are distinguished in the world of letters, and while the stakes were high, the game was relaxed and the humor scintillating.

One bright spring morning about eleven o'clock the membership, unshaven and bleary eyed, staggered out into the street, and the first thing their eyes hit upon was a bright-faced boy accompanied by his governess. Frank Adams (F.P.A.) looked at the smiling boy and, turning to his companions, remarked, "Imagine keeping a child that age out until this hour!"

CHAPTER IV

How to Play Poker: The Game's General Principles

A POKER POT might well be compared to a building. First we have the ground on which the building is located, or the ante; then we have the foundation, or first-round bets; then the middle structure, or early-round bets; and finally the superstructure, or last-round bets.

A beginner at poker should have a sound foundation at all times. The very best poker players do not always have this sound foundation, but if you sit in back of a good player for an evening, you will be surprised to see on how few bad hands he wastes even one chip; and when he does waste this one chip it is strictly for advertising purposes.

Then we come to the middle-game or main structure. If his hand is not developing as well as his opponents' hands seem to be, watch the good player abandon the few chips he has already put in the pot and get out quickly. The fact that his foundation may have been supersound means nothing to him if the middle-game developments are unfavorable to him and favorable to the other players. Remember, once a player puts chips into the pot, they cease to be his and merely represent an investment. If the investment starts to turn out badly, it is only a losing player who wastes more chips in an effort to protect it.

Finally we come to the superstructure, and here is where the expert really shines. Other players may build their foundation and middle structure just as well as the expert, but on those hands where a final large bet is called it will be found that the expert wins much more than half the time, while if a successful bluff is worked, the expert is much more likely to be on the right side of it than the ordinary player. The reason for this is that the expert is a psychologist. He is continually studying the other players to see, first, if they have any telltale habits, second, if there are any situations in which they act automatically.

In connection with general habits I divide poker players into three classes, namely: the ingenuous player, the tricky or coffee-housing player and the unreadable player.

The Ingenuous Player

When the ingenuous player looks worried he probably is worried. When he takes a long time to bet he probably doesn't think much of his hand. When he bets quickly he fancies his hand. When he bluffs he looks a little guilty, and when he really has a good hand you can see him mentally wishing to be called. This ingenuousness, incidentally, is seldom found in veterans. A player of this type usually quits poker at an early stage on account of his "bad luck."

The Tricky or Coffee-Housing Player

At least ninety per cent of all poker players fall into this category. The tricky player has a great tendency to act just the opposite of the way he really feels. Thus with a very good hand he trembles a little as he bets, while with a poor hand he fairly exudes confidence. Of course he may be triple-crossing, but year in and year out I have played in a great many games and have found that at least two times out of three when another player makes a special effort to look confident he has nothing, while when he tries to look nervous he is loaded.

There is one mild little coffee-housing habit that practically never fails to act as a giveaway. That is, showing too much nonchalance. For instance, it is my turn to bet and as I am about to put my chips in the pot one of the other players casually lights a cigarette. Experience tells me that this casual player is at least going to call me and is very likely to raise me if I bet. Accordingly, if I do see that sign, unless my hand is really very good I refuse to bet for him and simply check.

The Unreadable Player

This particular individual is, of course, the hardest opponent of all. Invariably he knows all the rules of correct play but departs from all of them on occasion. Unlike the ingenuous player, who acts the way he feels, or the coffee-houser, who acts the way he doesn't feel, this player has no consistency. Accordingly the fact that he exudes confidence or looks nervous gives no clue to the nature of his hand.

When there is such a player in the game I endeavor as much as possible to steer clear of him. But if I do find myself in a pot against him I have found one method which works reasonably well. That method is to relax completely and then see if some impression is conveyed to me in a subtle manner. Then, having secured this impression, I act directly against it. In other words, if the impression is that he is bluffing, I may drop; if the impression is that he has a good hand, I may call.

The preceding discussion has been of a very general nature. Here are a few specific giveaway habits I have noticed.[1]

Glancing to the Left

In the early stages of betting a player with a normal calling hand usually comes into the pot with no fuss whatsoever. However, a player with a good hand is going to consider raising and, before betting, is likely to cast a covert glance toward the players in back of him (on his left) to see if he can get any idea as to what they are going to do. If it looks to him as if two or three of them are going

[1]It should be borne in mind that poker has no ethics except in those cases referred to specifically in the chapter on How to Conduct Yourself in a Poker Game, and that short of actually cheating, which, by the way, includes attempting to peek at another player's hand, you have the right to any advantage you can gain.

to call, he sandbags; if it looks as if they are all going to drop out, he raises. Accordingly, when I see this glance, even though the player merely calls, I am fairly sure that his hand is fully strong enough for a raise.

Counting the Stacks

In a Table Stakes game when I see a man gazing intently at my chips I know he is counting them in order to see just how much he may win from or lose to me. If I have been doing the betting I know right at that point he is making up his mind whether to drop or to go through for the whole works. If he or someone else has been doing the betting, however, I now know that he is either planning some play against me or is afraid of some play I may make against him.

The following specific examples in Table Stakes Stud will show how advantage is taken of this.

I have one hundred chips in front of me. My first up card is an ace. I bet four chips. Only one player calls. On the next card I bet ten chips. Before calling he studies my stack. At this point I realize that he has a pair and has made up his mind to stay until the finish of that pot on the theory that I haven't got aces back to back. Accordingly, if I have aces back to back I go merrily ahead, betting twenty-five chips on the fourth round and the rest of the stack on the last; but if my ten-chip bet was in the nature of a bluff, I do not carry it any further.

Here is another example: I have a king up; the

player right in back of me has a jack, and another man has a queen. I bet a chip; both players call. On the second bet I check. The player with the jack bets five chips. Now if the man with the queen looks at both our stacks, I merely know he is estimating all possibilities; but if he pays particular attention to my stack and very little to my opponent's, I immediately mark him with queens back to back, the reason being that he is not worried about the man with the jack—he knows he has him beaten—but he is worried about me.

Looking at the Hole Card the Second Time

The very best Stud players, of course, look at their hole card once and then know it for the rest of the hand, but the average player, particularly with a low card in the hole, is likely to be careless and not remember it. Accordingly there are many instances where a second glance at the hole card gives a lot of information away.

For instance, the first bettor shows an ace; on the next card he receives a six and he promptly looks at his hole card. At this point there is a very strong presumption that his hole card is a six or something close to it.

Piling Chips on Your Hole Card

This is probably the most telltale giveaway habit of all. Before the second card is dealt a player looks at his hole card. If it is a low card he pays no attention to it, but if it is a high one he is quite likely to put it down and pile some chips on top of it immediately, to prevent any possibility of it blowing over. I know I must have seen chips piled on top of the hole card in that situation hundreds of times and I do not recall more than two or three instances when the card was lower than a jack and very few when it was not an ace or a king. I know from personal experience that other keen poker players have noticed this, as may be seen from the following story.

At a dinner party which was to be followed by a rather high Stud Poker game I was seated next to a very wealthy and opinionated man who considered himself a little tin god. He spent most of the dinnertime telling me not only what a great psychologist he was but also what poor psychologists all bridge experts were, the general tenor of his remarks being that all one needed to be a good bridge player was to learn a system and have a good memory, whereas a poker player needed psychology, nerve and ability to handle large amounts of chips.

It annoyed me and I decided that, if it was humanly possible, I would fix him in the coming poker game. Accordingly I deliberately differed with him at every point and acted as stupid as I possibly could. Then came the game. The first time I got an ace in the hole I piled my chips on top of it. The first time I got a king in the hole I piled my chips on top of it. And each succeeding time, for the first three hours of the game, I got an ace or king in the hole I continued the same practice.

By this time I knew that my dinner companion

had noticed this obvious giveaway and in fact had already taken advantage of it on one or two occasions, and I decided to begin my move against him. Accordingly I continued to pile my chips on an ace but stopped doing so when I had a king in the hole, and in order to conceal this from him I sometimes automatically threw my hand in. After about an hour of this I was finally rewarded. I had an eight-spot up and a king in the hole. He had a ten-spot up. A player with a queen opened. We both stayed. On the next card I drew a king; he drew a three. I bet. The player with the queen dropped and he raised. I called. On the next card we both drew four-spots. I checked; he bet. I called. On the final round I caught a seven; he drew a jack. I checked once more and he made a substantial bet, whereupon I tapped him. He called without a moment's hesitation, turned over a ten-spot he had in the hole and said gloatingly, "That's about the worst bluff I have ever seen, since I absolutely know that you cannot have a king in the hole."

Since I was really annoyed with him, I decided to prolong his agony and asked him in a faint voice how he knew this. He replied, "Because you have a bad habit. All evening, every time you got an ace or a king in the hole, you proceeded to pile chips on it. As I said at dinner, bridge players know nothing of psychology."

Turning over my hole card with one hand and reaching for the pot with the other, I merely remarked, "I still think you're mistaken."

Looking at Your Draw

In Draw Poker it is the exceptional player who will simply pick up the cards and look at them. The average player has various methods of mixing his draw with his hand, squeezing the cards, looking at one at a time, etc. While little can be learned about the nature of a player's hand from the manner in which he looks at his draw, there is one pretty general giveaway in connection with a one-card draw. A player drawing to a flush or to two pairs is likely to put the card he draws in the middle of his hand. A player drawing to an open straight invariably puts the card either on top or bottom. Accordingly, if a man takes a one-card draw and puts it in the center of his hand, I assume he is drawing to either a four flush or two pairs, and when he puts it on the end he is drawing to a straight.

Conditions of the Game

The conditions of the game are particularly valuable in determining how often you should depart from rules of correct technique. For instance, in a limit game it is probably sufficient to vary your game once or twice in an evening. In a Table Stakes game with a small ante and a great many chips on the table you can afford to play badly on all small pots in an effort to build up one big pot which will more than account for your earlier losses.

In a Table Stakes game it is particularly important to watch the chip situation of all players. In particular the most dangerous are the player with a lot of chips and the player with very few chips. Everyone knows enough to watch the player with a lot of chips since he is the person who can tap you at any time. But few people pay enough attention to the player with very few chips.

The danger represented by this player lies in the fact that he is likely to shove all his chips into the pot at any moment, whereas if he had a lot of chips he would not make such a play. Now if you are right in back of him and call, even though you are certain you have a better hand than the man who has bet, there is a distinct chance that someone in back of you will be able to raise. Now, since the first bettor has all his chips in the pot, he gets what is known as a "free ride," whereas if you want to try to draw out you must call the raise.

Incidentally, when we come to High-Low, where we give special rules for the division of side money, we will discuss this situation at greater length.

The technique of varying the size of your own bets is very important. For instance, let's suppose we are playing a Table Stakes game. In an early stage I decide to start bluffing, and when it comes to the last card I have one opponent and there are about two hundred chips in the pot. I can be certain my opponent has a pair of fives. I have been trying to convey the impression that I have a pair of jacks. I know this man can be bluffed, else I would not have started that particular play against him. Therefore I decide to bet, and my problem is whether to bet approximately the size of the pot or substantially more or less, and here it is my knowledge of my opponent that determines.

Against one type of player I would be likely to bet only a hundred chips. He would be likely to say to himself, "Jacoby surely has a pair of jacks and wants me to call, but I won't." The same man, however, will quickly call a three-hundred- or four-hundred-chip bet, figuring that I definitely am trying to bluff him. Another type man, however, would be sure to call a one-hundred-chip bet, reasoning that I was afraid to bet more, but he would drop before a three-hundred- or four-hundred-chip bet. Finally there is a third type of player who always figures that any variation from the normal indicates a bluff. Against that man I would bet exactly the size of the pot.

Of course my readers may now ask, "How about the man whom you can't figure out at all?" To which my answer is that I do not try to outplay him. I merely trust to luck. Fortunately there are not too many of that breed.

Just as you may vary the size of your own bets to fit different conditions, so you should carefully study the significance of any variation by an opponent. Offhand there is a presumption that the larger the bet the better the hand. But, as explained before, a good player may well be reversing this practice and making a small bet with a tremendous hand or a very large bet as a bluff.

However, here is one instance where an abnormally large bet practically always means an abnormally large hand and should act as a definite warning. The game is Jack Pots and the general custom of that particular game is for the opener to bet either two or three chips. However, a player suddenly opens for six chips. Right at that point it is good policy to assume that the reason for the large bet is a large hand and to beware.

Luck

"Patience and per-*sev*-erance
Made a Bishop of his Reverence."[2]

In any one session of poker the Goddess of Chance is the one who determines the winners and the losers. In two or three sessions she has a lot to say about who wins. But over a long period she bestows her favors equally, and the good players win and the poor players lose.

A poker player might well divide his game into two parts: (1) the psychology, already discussed in this chapter; (2) the technical. I have already mentioned the fact that the really good poker player must depart from correct technical play sufficiently often so that his opponents can never be certain as to what he is doing. Nevertheless, the technical side is far more important than the other; and while correct technical play will not make you a winner, it will certainly keep you from being much of a loser even against the best poker players in the world.

[2]An old friend, the late Spottswood Bowers of New York City, loved to relax at poker but he did not believe in throwing away his chips recklessly, and occasionally, when reproached for tight playing, would repeat the above appropriate lines.

As an example let us take a Table Stakes Stud game in which Player A starts with aces back to back and Player B starts with kings back to back. If B is a great psychologist he may decide at some stage that A has aces and get out of the pot before he is hurt too badly. If he is merely a technician he will go through to the end, lose his chips and complain about his bad luck quite properly. But this bad luck is not going to afflict him often.

Now let us consider Player C who starts in the Stud game with a nine in the hole and a ten-spot up, against a player who shows an ace. Player C now draws a nine for his third card and promptly proceeds to lose all his chips because the other man started with aces backed up. C also complains about his bad luck but he has no right to. When he stayed against the ace, in the first place, he was violating the correct technical procedure and hence directly caused his own misfortune.

This habit of staying with inadequate hands merely to give yourself a little more action is one that no amount of psychological skill can hope to overcome against good players, although against bad players you can get away with almost anything. Of course the average player who trails along without having cards to justify it knows he is doing something wrong, but says to himself: "Well, it won't hurt just this once." But he doesn't do it just once—he does it tens and hundreds of times. Remember, one hundred chips wasted one at a time are nevertheless one hundred chips.

Bucking Your Luck

Suppose you owe a man twenty-five dollars and go to him and say, "Let's toss a coin to see whether I pay you fifty or nothing." You are offering a fair proposition, but he now says, "No. I'd rather collect the twenty-five." "All right," you reply. "Let's toss a coin to see whether I pay you one hundred dollars or nothing."

Right away my readers will remark, "There's no one crazy enough to offer that proposition." However, a great many of the poker players I have seen—in fact, I think a majority—do exactly that in a different manner by bucking their luck when they are losing. And when they once start bucking their luck they are usually giving the other players, who are playing their hands properly, much better odds than the man who offers three to one on an even proposition.

When I am losing in a poker game I say to myself, "I can get even when, if and as my luck turns. If it doesn't turn today it will tomorrow. Meanwhile I am not going to force matters with bad hands."

Of course there are times when I do overplay my cards, and a casual observer who happened to play poker with me might think, "This Jacoby doesn't play according to his book, but instead frequently stays in the pot in situations where he recommends dropping and raises in situations where he recommends calling."

However, a closer observer would notice that this liberality occurs only when I am winning and able to be liberal with someone else's money. In other words, I am not bucking my bad luck but I am pushing my good luck.

Tight vs Loose Play

In my discussion of individual poker games invariably I give rules as to the minimum holding with which a player should stay in a pot. I am certain that the average good player of these games will say, "Jacoby's requirements are entirely too stringent, and actually I can afford to play more liberally than he recommends."

The good players will be right in their own particular case, but it must be borne in mind that this book is written for all classes of poker players, and the student or novice, or even the good player playing a game which is new to him, will do well to play even tighter than I recommend.

The general tone of the play in any game affects your requirements for staying. For instance, I know of two Seven-Card High-Low games in one of which no one ever stays without two very low cards and the first-round raise nearly always indicates a holding such as the two, three and seven of the same suit. In that game if you don't play approximately as tight as the other players you have absolutely no chance to come out anything but a loser. In another game everybody stays to draw a fourth card, people raise blind, and one can afford to play in that game much more liberally than I recommend. Of course a tight player could win in that game with absolute certainty, but he would never be asked to play again, since the whole purpose of that group is to have a very exciting time with plenty of action for all players, and they are not going to support a man who sits back and waits.

Bluffing

The technique of bluffing depends materially on what game is being played. Thus in a Limit game the player who bluffs should not really expect to drive his opponents out very often, and in that game your bluffs correspond to an advertising appropriation and should be made just often enough so that your opponents will call you when you really have the best hand. (Note of warning: The average player who does bluff in a Limit game does so entirely too often.)

In a Table Stakes game, while your bluffs also have a slight advertising value, they are frequently planned with the serious idea of winning the pot and constitute perhaps the most spectacular maneuver in poker. Some of these bluffs may be made on the spur of the moment or they may be planned well in advance of when they come off.

In planning such a bluff the first consideration is a psychological analysis of the other players. For instance, the average player who is a big loser will usually call any bet out of sheer desperation. But a minority, once they get well in the hole, are afraid to lose much more and hence are a cinch to bluff.

About half the people I have played with are easy to bluff when they are big winners, since they say to themselves, "Why risk part of my profit?" The other half are almost unbluffable, since they feel it is a sporting gesture to throw in their chips and call.

The least likely victim for a bluff, however, is the player who after being a winner has suddenly reached the point where he is a small loser, since he will call, knowing that if you are bluffing he is once more ahead of the game. Conversely, the man who after being loser for a long while has finally pulled himself ahead of the game is the best victim, since he is not likely to want to risk his profit.

Finally, the most successful bluff is likely to be the innocent one. For instance, a player who has mistaken a heart for a diamond may think he has a flush and act so convincingly that everybody will drop. Then there is the case of the American playing in a very high-stake game in China with the help of an interpreter. On the first hand the American picked up the king, queen, jack and ten of diamonds and an odd card The first player said, "Ah foy," and the interpreter explained, "He opens the pot for five hundred dollars."

The American put in five hundred dollars, and the next player said, "Ah moy." "He raises a thousand," translated the interpreter. The dealer now said, "Ah goy," meaning, the interpreter explained, "He raises five thousand."

The betting continued some time with the American always calling. He drew one card; the opener checked, and the American checked without looking at his hand. The next player said, "Ah woy," and the interpreter announced, "It's a bet of twenty-five thousand dollars." A couple of players called, and now the American, shuffling his cards thoroughly, spread his hand slowly and saw the deuce of spades. Banging the cards down on the table, he exclaimed, "Ah hell!"

One after another the Chinamen threw their hands away, and the interpreter said, "Your one-million-dollar bluff won the pot!"

CHAPTER V

Draw Poker

Jack Pots

When to Open

When the game is five handed or less you should make it a point to open the pot with any legal openers. With six in the game the first player should pass a pair of jacks or queens. Anyone else with such a pair should open. With seven in the game the first two players should pass jacks or queens, and in an eight-handed game the first three should pass. With a pair of kings or better it is always worth while opening the pot.

The reason for the above apparently arbitrary rules lies in the fact that with only four players to hear from, the chances are that no one will stay or raise, and that by opening the pot you will win the ante. With more players to hear from, the chance that someone will come in becomes relatively greater. Hence you need additional protection and should not open on an absolute minimum.

Sandbagging

Sandbagging occurs when a player who has a good hand, such as three of a kind or a straight, decides to pass in the hope that someone else will open. In this event the sandbagger intends to raise. If there are five or less in the game there is no great point in sandbagging, since you run too great a risk that the hand will be passed out. With seven or eight in the game, however, it will frequently prove profitable for the first or even the second bettor to do this. True, the hand may be passed out, but the chance of this happening is much less than in the four- or five-handed game.

In deciding to sandbag, your exact holding is important. For instance, suppose you have three deuces, a three and a four. The other players' hands must be made up from the other forty-seven cards, and the chances that one of them will have a pair of jacks or better is much greater than it would be if you, for example, held three aces, a king and a queen.

Accordingly, we may establish as our principle that the time to sandbag is when you have three of a kind or better, when there are at least five players to act after you and when your hand is made up of low cards.

Staying-On Possibilities After the Pot Is Opened

It is fairly common to hold four cards to a straight or flush and a fifth card which does not match. Here there is a great temptation to stay in the pot and draw to your straight or flush. The mathematics of this are as follows:

(a) *Drawing to a flush*. You have five cards in your hand. Hence there are forty-seven cards missing, of which nine will make your flush for you. Your chance is nine in forty-seven or just less than one in five.

(b) *Drawing to a straight open at both ends*. There are eight cards which will help you. Hence your chance is eight in forty-seven or just over one in six.

(c) *Drawing to an inside straight*. There are four cards that will help you and your chance of success is four in forty-seven or one in twelve.

Our first rule is: never draw to an inside straight since your chance of filling is but one in twelve. Consider the sad fate of the old farmer who used to play poker once a week and kept drawing to inside straights. He eventually had to mortgage his farm, but he still kept drawing to inside straights and finally he caught one. Unfortunately someone else made a full house at the same time, and bang went the whole farm.

In drawing to an open-end straight, since your chance of success is but one in six, you ought to be getting five to one odds in order to make it worth while to risk your money. Accordingly, unless the ante is large in proportion to the bet, you should only draw to a straight when there are at least four other people in the pot. Furthermore, we refer you to our farmer friend. There is no guarantee that if you make your straight you are going to win the pot.

In drawing to a flush you have one chance in five of succeeding and, furthermore, a somewhat better chance of winning the pot in the event that you make your flush than if you make your straight. Accordingly, we recommend drawing to a flush when there are as many as two other people in the pot or when the ante is large.

Incidentally, these recommendations of ours are slightly more liberal than the mathematical percentages would appear to warrant. The reason for this lies in the fact that if you do not make a practice of drawing to flushes and straights when you can, the other players will know that when you draw one card you must surely have two pairs and will take due advantage of that knowledge.

Staying with a Pair

The chance of improving when you draw three cards to a pair is only two in seven. From this it should be apparent that there is seldom any point in staying on a pair of tens or less. You know the opener has a better hand than you, and in addition he has just as good a chance to improve as you have. Similarly a pair of jacks are no good for purposes of staying and a pair of queens doubtful. With aces, kings or better you should stay.

When to Raise

If the pot is opened by one of the first players and you are the following bettor, there is no point in raising. If you have a very good hand, there is always a chance that someone else will raise, whereupon you can raise back, and if your hand is not very good, anybody who now comes in is likely to have a better hand than you and those with weaker hands than yours will drop out.

In all other situations you should raise in accordance with the following requirements:

(a) If the pot is opened by one of the later players and no one else has stayed, raise on any two pairs. The chances are that the opener has but one pair.

(b) If the pot is opened under the guns, raise with nines up or better. The reason why you need a better hand here is due to the fact that the man who opens under the guns surely has not done so on a pair of queens or jacks and hence is much more likely to have two pairs or three of a kind than the man who has opened in a later position.

The fact that one or more people stay in the pot should not change the requirements for raising, except that here you must use your judgment. Beware of raising the bet where a player who makes a habit of lying in wait comes in. You are likely to run into a re-raise.

Subsequent Raises

The second raise should indicate at least three of a kind or possibly aces up. The third raise a minimum of three kings; the fourth raise a high straight; the fifth raise a high flush; the sixth raise a full house; the seventh raise a big full house; the eighth raise four of a kind. Eleven raises are about as many as you should ever see before the draw in a good poker game. Of course in very liberal games these raises and re-raises are made on much weaker hands than the ones I have listed.

Staying After a Raise

If you have already bet, you should plan to stay after a raise if you have any more than the minimum or if you have reason to suspect that the man who has raised is bluffing. If you have not already bet, you should drop out unless you believe that your hand is as good as that of the last raiser. In particular there is no point at all in entering a raised pot on an open-end straight and very little point in entering on a four flush.

The reason for this may be shown mathematically as follows:

Assume a seven-handed game, a one-chip ante and a five-chip limit. The total ante is seven chips. The pot is opened for five chips and two people stay. You now call on a four flush. When you put your five chips in there are already twenty-two chips in the pot. You are getting twenty-two to five odds for your money. However, if the pot has been raised, let us assume you call and the opener and the other players stay for the raise. You are now putting ten chips into the pot. The other players have put in thirty, and you are now getting thirty-seven to ten odds. Instead of getting four and one half to one you are getting just better than three and one half to one. Furthermore, there is a chance that some player may not stay for the raise, in which case your odds are reduced, or there may be a further raise.

Finally, the chance that your straight or flush, if made, will win a raised pot is not as great as that of winning a pot where no one is strong enough to raise.

Drawing to Your Hand

In general it is good policy to draw down to your hand, i.e., if you have three of a kind to start with you draw two cards; if you have two pairs, one card; if you have one pair you draw three cards. However, a great majority of players who have three of a kind like to conceal this by taking one card only. Most of the time this is good poker but it should not be an invariable rule. There is no point in standing pat with two pairs unless you desire to bluff, and the main purpose in holding a third card with one pair is to convey the impression that you may have three of a kind.

The winning poker player will vary his draw. Occasionally he will hold a kicker to a pair, while with three of a kind he will draw one card about once in four times and two cards the other three quarters of the time.

Incidentally, I want to tell the case of a man I know who always loses at Draw Poker. Nevertheless he thinks he plays very well. He has one great weakness in that he always holds a kicker to a pair or three of a kind. The result of this is that he materially reduces his chances of improving his hand and at the same time actually gains nothing in deception, because the other players all know that when he draws two cards he has a pair and a kicker and not three of a kind.

Pass Out[1]

When to Pass Out

If you have no pair, no open-end straight and no four flush, there is no point in your betting even one chip.

When to Open for One Chip

With a small pair, four flush or open-end straight, or a hand strong enough to sandbag, open with one chip. (Note: With a pair of sixes or less a conservative player will do well to drop out if he is one of the first hands in a large game, the reason being that there is a good chance he will be raised, whereupon his hand is not strong enough to call.)

When to Open with Several Chips

Any time you would open if the game were Jack Pots you should open for a substantial bet. Furthermore, after several people pass out ahead of you, you may weaken these requirements and make a real bet with a pair of tens or nines.

When to Raise

You should raise a one-chip bet with any hand with which you would open a jack pot. Similarly, if a real bet has been made, you may assume the man who made the real bet has about the same strength as if he had opened a jack pot and base your procedure on the principles stated under Jack Pots.

[1]So called because there is no checking allowed before the draw.

Anything Opens

The technique of this game is very similar to that of Jack Pots, the only difference being that there is slightly more sandbagging. The reason for this is, of course, that in this game, when five or six players check, someone may open with a small pair or even with nothing, in the hopes of being able to steal the pot. Hence, since fewer hands are passed out than in Jack Pots, more players will pass a good hand in the hope of catching a victim.

Blind Opening

The Blind Opening game is designed for one purpose—that is, to force everyone to play liberally. Usually the ante is large and the limit small. As a result, anyone stays with an open-end straight or a four flush, and unless the bet is raised a player will come in with any pair. Furthermore, a man with as good as a pair of jacks will raise, and a man with two pairs will give a second raise, so that whereas we mentioned eleven raises are all you can expect before the draw in Jack Pots, in the Blind Opening game it is not at all unusual to see as many as twenty raises before the draw and then find that no one has better than a straight.

Betting After the Draw

The betting after the draw is about the same in all forms of Draw Poker. Each player will have a good idea from the previous betting as to the mean-

ing of each other player's draw and will base his
betting after the draw on what he holds and what
he expects his opponents to hold. However, there
are a few general rules that are well worth giving
here:

1. Don't bet into a one-card draw. When a
player draws one card there is an excellent chance
that he is drawing to make a straight or a flush.
If this is the case and he fails to improve, he will
not call your bet and you have gained nothing.
If he has improved he will raise you, and you will
have lost the amount of your bet plus the additional chips you are likely to bet in order to find
out whether or not he is bluffing.

Even though there has been no one-card draw
it is pretty good tactics to make a habit of checking
if you are the opener, since by so doing you ef-
fectively conceal whether or not your hand has
improved. When you do bet after the draw it
should indicate either that you have improved
your hand slightly or that you figure your original
hand was good enough to stand a call or, finally,
that you are bluffing.

Play of Two Pairs

Once in every twenty-one deals a player is fortunate or unfortunate enough, as the case may be,
to hold two pairs, and it is the play of this particular hand more than any other which determines
the winners and the losers in a limit game of Draw
Poker.

With one pair you are more or less protected by the weakness of your hand, and with three of a kind, or better, by its strength. As a matter of fact two pairs is also a very strong hand before the draw, but it must be borne in mind that the only hand it can improve to is a full house, and the chance of getting your full house is but one in twelve. Accordingly there is a carefully followed maxim in poker that with two pairs you should raise before the draw, since you cannot afford to raise after the draw.

The primary reason for this raise is that chances are you have the best hand and you want to discourage competition as much as possible, thereby giving yourself the best possible chance of winning the pot. However, the average poker player follows this adage blindly and all the time. This is a distinct mistake, particularly if your two pairs are very small. Remember, there is an excellent chance that the opener, particularly if he has opened under the guns, also has two pairs or better.

Now, since your two pairs are small, the chances are that the opener's hand will be better than yours. And if several people are in the pot there is a distinct likelihood that one of them may be sandbagging. Hence, since the odds are twelve to one against improvement, there is no point in your starting to build up a big pot for someone else.

Of course if you feel reasonably certain that no other player has as good a hand as you, it is good tactics to raise. True, with several people in the pot the chances are that one will draw out against you; but the odds you are getting for your money are much better than this chance.

Another advantage of not raising with two pairs after several people come into the pot lies in the fact that now, if you draw one card, the other players are more than likely to assume that you are drawing to a straight or a flush, and if you do make your full house and someone else makes a high flush, you will get a far better play than if you had raised before the draw.

A very interesting question in the play of two pairs is when, if ever, to throw one of them away. This play in poker roughly corresponds to the Grand Coup in contract. I know the Grand Coup well—in fact six years ago I actually made it. Similarly I expect someday to throw away the smaller of two pairs but have never yet found the right time. However, I do remember my father telling me how he made the play once under the following circumstances:

The game was Jack Pots with a limit. Player A opened the pot. Father raised, holding a pair of fours, a pair of twos and an ace. Player A now stayed for the raise and drew one card. This marked him with two good-sized pairs since Father was sure he would have raised back with aces up or three of a kind. Hence Father proceeded to throw away his pair of deuces and hold a pair of fours and an ace. On this draw his chance of making aces up or better was one in five—a much better chance than the one in twelve of making a full house on a one-card draw. Sure enough, Father caught an ace and with aces up won the pot.

Incidentally, without the ace it would have been good tactics to draw three cards, although the percentage would not have been nearly so good as when holding the ace kicker.

The Block System

The purpose of this type of Draw Poker, played in St Louis and many other Middle Western and Southern cities, is to create plenty of action and at the same time put the "tight" player at a disadvantage rather than at an advantage, as he is in most poker games.

As a starter the dealer places twenty-five chips in the pot, representing a nineteen-chip ante, a two-chip blind opening by the player at his left and a raise to four chips by the second player. The third player now has the right to make the first actual bet, and he may either call the four chips or raise to six. The limit a player may raise before the draw is two chips, and as each player raises he announces what he is raising to. Thus the first player to raise says, "Six"; the second, "Eight"; etc.

After the draw the limit for any one raise is the total amount bet by each player before the draw. Thus if the last raise before the draw was to twelve chips, the limit after the draw is twelve chips; if the last raise was to twenty, the limit is twenty chips.

In order to increase competition Dogs and Tigers (see p. 137–138 of the Laws) are counted in addition to regular poker hands. Therefore, in addition to four flushes and open-end straights, there are any number of hands which present attractive possibilities before the draw, including a new one—the twelve-chance hand. For example, a player with a king, jack, ten and nine may draw an ace and make a Big Dog, a queen and make a straight, or an eight and make a Big Tiger.

Since it apparently costs the first player four chips to come into the pot and there are already twenty-five there, he figures he is getting better than six to one for his money and is encouraged to stay on any eight-chance hand or a small pair. Subsequently, anybody with a twelve-chance hand, a four flush, two pairs or even a pair of aces or kings is likely to raise. In actuality a liberal player with two good-sized pairs or a twelve-chance hand is likely to raise the pot as many as ten or twelve times, particularly if there are five or six others in it. Furthermore, once a player starts in a pot at all, since the raises are only two chips at a time, he is likely to stay right through to the bitter end on the theory that the particular raise he is faced with will be the last. Accordingly, in playing this game you should bear in mind that when you put four or six chips in the pot to start with, it is about ten to one that someone will raise, about five to one that someone will raise back and better than even money that you will have to pay at least twelve chips to get the privilege of drawing. Therefore the wise player, before betting his four chips, says to himself: "Am I willing to bet twelve?"

Here are my own requirements, which I find work out pretty well:

1. If I am one of the first two players I come in only

    (a) If I have a pair of jacks or better;

    (b) If I have a twelve-chance hand or a four flush;

    (c) If I have an eight-way chance to make a Tiger or Big Dog.

It should be specifically noted that I do not come in as first or second bettor when I have an eight-way chance to make a straight or Little Dog but do come in when I have the same chance of making a Tiger or Big Dog. The reason for this lies in the fact that invariably there will be several other people in the pot drawing to possibilities. Accordingly, if I make a straight and one of them makes a Dog or a Tiger, all that happens is that my success in the draw costs me additional chips. But if I make a Tiger and they make a Dog or a straight, I really show a profit.

Incidentally, in drawing to a holding such as ace, king, queen and nine or ace, king, queen and ten, you always have a slight additional possibility— namely, that you will make a high pair and that the high pair will win the pot.

2. If I am the last man to act and there is no raise, I come in on any pair or eight-chance hand, since in this position the only person with a chance to raise me is the blind opener.

3. In intermediate positions my requirements are less than if I am first or second but more than if I am last.

4. If I am the blind opener and by some miracle no one has raised, I stay even though I have to make a five-card draw.

Going into a Raised Pot

If there has been but one raise before my turn to act, I usually come in if I would have come in in first position. If there have been two raises, I want to have at least a pair of kings, a four flush or a twelve-chance hand.

Raising

Except when you are the first or second man to act, in which case it is pretty good policy simply to trail along and wait for someone else to raise, you should raise with a pair of kings, any twelve-chance hand and, if as many as five other players are in the pot, with a four flush. With one pair you should not figure on raising again. With any other of these raising hands it is pretty good policy to give at least one more raise if you are raised back.

In raising with a made hand, two big pairs are usually worth four raises; three of a kind, six; a big three of a kind, eight; and a pat hand, ten or more. In raising on possibilities you should stop fairly quickly. Thus a four flush is worth only two raises, and a twelve-chance hand, three to six. The number of raises which a twelve-chance hand is worth is naturally based on what you are drawing to. For instance, suppose you hold a two, three, four and five. An ace or a six will give you a straight, which, however, will lose to any other pat hand; while a seven will give you the smallest kind of Little Dog. Therefore, in drawing to this hand you must bear in mind that even though you make it you are likely to lose the pot. However, in drawing to a king, jack, ten and nine, a queen gives you a high straight, an ace a Big Dog, and an eight a Big Tiger, and you realize that if you make this hand your chance of winning the pot is pretty good.

Bluffing

In spite of the extreme liberality with which this game is always played there is plenty of scope for bluffing. The pat-hand bluff is of particular value. In this instance you raise indefinitely before the draw, stand pat and then bet immediately. Of course if someone else has made himself a real pat hand in the draw, he is going to call you. Otherwise you have a very good chance of getting away with the pot.

Stakes

If a group has been playing regular Draw Poker and wishes to try this game, my suggestion is that they keep the same nominal stakes but settle for one third or one quarter, the reason for this being that the number of chips usually lost in this game is about three or four times as many as in regular Draw Poker.

Bluffing at Draw Poker

In Limit Draw Poker, and practically all Draw Poker is played with a limit, a player should regard his bluffs in the same manner as a businessman regards his advertising appropriation. During the course of a session of play you have a certain number of winning hands. Naturally you bet with these hands and naturally you want people to call you, since when they call they are giving you chips. However, if you never bluff, no one is going to call these bets, and hence you should spend a certain amount of money bluffing in order to get these calls. Of course once in a while a bluff will be successful and will win the pot for you. That is just gravy, since you should bear in mind that your bluffs are actually nothing but advertising.

The most elementary and frequent bluff in Draw Poker is the bluff when you have drawn to a straight or flush and failed to make it. As a matter of fact practically every player bluffs too often in this situation since the temptation is so great. Actually you should bluff about once for every ten or fifteen times you draw to this hand unsuccessfully. When you bluff more often in this situation you are putting too much money into your advertising budget. When you bluff less often you are going to lose a lot of calls when you have made your hand.

The pat-hand bluff is one of the most effective I know and is really very likely to succeed. There are three forms to this bluff. First the pot is opened right in front of you and you simply call. Now if anyone raises, you stand pat, and immediately all the other players think you surely have a pat hand and are sandbagging. After the draw you bet the limit, and it really takes a stout heart to call you.

The second variation: you raise before the draw and again stand pat. This second variation is by no means so advantageous as the first. Here is why: we will assume a total ante of seven chips and a five-chip limit. In the first instance the pot is opened for five chips. We call for five, leaving a total of seventeen in the pot. No one else comes in. After the draw we bet five more. If we are called, the bluff costs us ten chips; if we are not called, we have gained twelve. In the second instance there is a chance that the opener will drop when we raise. However, assuming that he does stay, there are more chips in the pot. Hence he is more likely to call us after the draw. Furthermore, if this bluff is unsuccessful, we have lost fifteen chips.

The third variation of the pat-hand bluff occurs when you open, someone raises and you now decide to raise back, stand pat and bet after the draw. In Jack Pots this particular technique is likely to prove effective since your opponent will know that you have openers, at least, and therefore will say to himself: "If he didn't really have a pat hand, why wouldn't he try to draw against me?"

A favorite bluff of many players is to raise on a four flush. They then draw one card and bet, whether they make their flush or not. While this bluff must lose money in itself, the player who makes it gets an awful lot of calls when he starts with two big pairs or three of a kind and uses the same tactics.

In addition to the above there are any number of complicated bluffing situations in many of which a player will actually get away with the pot, particularly if he makes his bluff against a good player of the cautious type. For instance, here is one example: Players A and B stay in a raised pot and each draws one card. After the draw Player A bets and Player B raises, whereupon there is a strong presumption that Player B has at least a high straight. Player A now raises back, purely as a bluff. Player B says to himself: "A must have at least a full house to raise me back," and throws away his hand.

CHAPTER VI

Stud Poker

WHEN STUD IS PLAYED PROPERLY real competition
occurs in less than one hand in ten and furthermore, when this real competition does occur, it is
usually restricted to two players. As a result, ordinary Stud is more of a gambling game than a light
pastime.

However, for those who want to play it there are
six basic rules which should be followed almost
implicitly. If you do follow them, there is no guarantee that you will win, but if you do not follow them,
you are certain to lose. They are:

Rule I. Do not stay on the first round unless:

(a) You have a pair.

(b) Your hole card outranks any card shown.

(c) Your hole card is as good as any card showing and your up card is a nine-spot or higher.

Exception: Once in a while, if both your hole
card and up card are higher than any card showing
except that of the original bettor, you may stay.

Rule II. Do not stay if you are beaten in sight.

In other words, suppose you stay with a nine-spot showing and a king in the hole. On the second round you draw a ten-spot and some other player draws an ace. Right at this point you should give up all interest in the pot, the reason being that:

(a) If you don't improve you can't beat the ace.

(b) If you do improve, the man with the ace may improve also and will still beat you.

(c) And, most important, the man with the ace showing may have an ace in the hole. Whereupon, if you catch a pair, your bad stay is really going to prove expensive.

Exception: In a Table Stakes game where you have already wagered substantially more than half your money, or in a Limit game where you have already wagered the limit bet several times, you may violate this rule. It's simply a matter of percentage.

Example: You have twenty-five chips in front of you in a Table Stakes game and an ace in the hole. On round one the bet is five chips. On round two the bet is fifteen chips. On round three a player now shows a pair of deuces. You have made no pair. Nevertheless you should stay for your remaining five chips. After all, the player with the deuces very likely has no other pair. And while the chances are greatly against your improving, you are getting very good odds for your money. Furthermore, you are safe from the great danger of the man who stays optimistically—namely, if you do improve and the other man still has an "immortal," you can't lose any more since all your money is in.

Rule III. On the fifth card, if you show the best hand, check—do not bet. The reasons for this are:

(a) No player who can't beat what you show is going to call.

(b) If you have nothing extra in the hole and anyone calls you, he will have you beaten.

(c) If you do have an "immortal" and check, someone may bet into you and give you a chance to raise him back; if you bet, the best you can hope for is a call.

Exception: If your hole card helps your hand but is not good enough to give you an "immortal," there are times when you can afford to vary this rule. For instance: you started with an ace up and a six in the hole and subsequently drew a four, six and eight. The only other player in the pot started with a five up and subsequently drew a king, ten and three. There is a very good chance that his hole card is a five or an ace. If you check, he is not likely to bet into you; but if you bet into him and he happens to have a five or an ace in the hole, he is quite likely to call on the theory that you are bluffing.

Rule IV. Do not bet into a possible "immortal" when the player with the possible "immortal" can raise you back.

Example: You are playing in a Table Stakes game and on the last card hold a pair of kings, one of which is concealed. There are two hundred chips in the pot and you have five hundred chips in front of you. The player who shows an ace checks. You bet two hundred chips. Everyone else drops, and now the man with the ace raises you the balance of your chips. You either have to drop or, if you think he is bluffing, you must pay the rest of your chips.

On the other hand, take the same situation when you have but two hundred chips in front of you. Now you can bet your two hundred chips since you cannot be raised. True, you can lose your two hundred chips but you can't lose any more.

Rule V. The correct bet is the size of the pot.

When you bet less you make it too easy for people to stay, and when you bet more you immediately drive out all but the very good hands. Now someone will say to himself, "If I happen to have a very good hand, why should I not bet less than the size of the pot in order to keep as many people in as possible?" The theory of this is fine. In practice it is no good because it doesn't take your opponents long to find out this interesting little habit of yours, with the result that any time you make an abnormally small bet they draw right into their shells.

When playing with a limit you should bet the size of the pot until such time as the chips in the pot exceed the limit. From then on you should bet the limit.

Rule VI. It is also considered unwise to reveal your hole card in this game.

In connection with revealing your hole card there are two amusing stories. The first concerns the almost fabulous group of the Roaring Twenties, known as the Sons of Hope, who played Table Stakes Stud for one-hundred-thousand-dollar stacks and up. One day they are on their way to Florida in a private car, and the game, if anything, is larger than usual. One of the Sons of Hope, with a pair of kings back to back, has just tapped another for three hundred thousand dollars. The other player, who has a pair of queens, is considering calling. At this point the man with the kings has a fit of coughing and blows his hole card over. Following a moment of silence, he remarks, "Dammit! I should have bought the Smith Brothers Cough Drop factory last week. This would have paid for it!"

The other story comes from Harpo Marx. Harpo was playing in a reasonably sized game and had kings back to back. A player on the other side of the table, showing the ace of spades, tapped; and Harpo, for some reason or other, took a long time to make up his mind what to do. The other player became impatient, turned over his four exposed cards and held all five in his hand, saying, "Come on. Make up your mind." Harpo then said, "Don't rush me. And, what's more, put your cards back where I can see them." The other player obligingly complied, but this time the ace of clubs appeared instead of the ace of spades, so Harpo's problem was solved.

The preceding rules should be followed whether you are playing with a table-stake or flat limit. In other situations, however, the type of game you are playing must influence your procedure greatly, and we will discuss Table Stakes and Limit Stud separately.

Table Stakes

Initial Bet

In some Stud games the player with the high card is required to bet on the first round. In others he may pass. Even though allowed to pass, it is good policy to bet if you are high, irrespective of what your hole card is. The reason for this is that a large proportion of the really big pots occur when the first bettor has a pair back to back and someone else with a smaller pair starts raising early. However, if a player makes a habit of passing when his hole card is no good, he immediately serves notice any time he makes an initial bet that in addition to the fact that he shows a higher card than anyone else his hole card also possesses merit. Other players, knowing this, are going to be particularly careful and not start raising. Hence he loses all chance at very big pots.

Raising on the First Card

In general there is little to be gained by raising on the first card. If you do have a pair back to back or an ace in the hole you can afford to wait to see how things develop.

However, the winning player must vary his game. Hence on occasion you should raise on the first card. This raise may be made when you have a pair back to back, when you have an ace or king in the hole or even as a pure bluff.

However, like all positive maneuvers in poker, you should be sure the stage is properly set. My own practice is to raise under the following three conditions:

(1) My up card outranks any card on the table except that of the original bettor.

(2) At least two players have already called the original bet.

(3) There is not more than one player in back of me.

The reasons for each of these three conditions are:

(a) There is a distinct chance that my raise will drive the opponent out. In that event my up card becomes the highest on the table and I have a distinct advantage against the remaining players.

(b) Since this play is made with the hope that the opener will drop, there is no point in making it unless I have at least two potential customers.

(c) It is always unsound to raise when there are several players who have not acted.

It will be noted that in discussing this first-card raise I have made no mention of my hole card, the reason being that if I make this raise I may have a pair back to back or I may have a deuce in the hole, and furthermore, even though I have a pair back to back and all three conditions are met with, I still may not raise. After all, remember the principle of variation: No player can make any rule invariable and win at poker.

Second-Round Betting

While the really big bets, if any, come in the third and fourth rounds, it is usually the second round that lays the foundation; and if there is no real action then, it is very unlikely that the betting will get into telephone numbers later on. Here there is plenty of opportunity for deception. For instance, the high man nearly always bets, and his failure to do so means one of two things: (a) he has nothing at all in the hole, or (b) he has his hole card paired up and is trying to catch himself a fish. Which situation is the case becomes a matter of observation and outguessing the other fellow.

When you stay with a high card in the hole it is always nice to pair it immediately. However, when you do pair it immediately, remember the other players are going to suspect you. For instance, suppose on the first round the high card is a queen and bets a chip; you stay with a deuce up and a king in the hole and now catch a king. The other players know in advance that with the deuce up you would not have stayed without either a deuce, king or ace in the hole and hence immediately suspect that now you have a pair of kings. A small bet or none at all at this point is certainly likely to act as a warning signal, while a bet the size of the pot is likely to find practically everyone dropping out, maybe with one customer remaining. In this situation I have found that an unusually large bet is very likely to coax a call. For instance, suppose there are seven chips in the pot; I bet a dozen. Now a player with a moderate-sized pair is likely to say to himself: "Jacoby had a pair of deuces originally and is trying to protect that pair of deuces by betting right out; I will call." Once he calls that twelve-chip bet I really have him hooked.

On the next round I may bet as many as fifty chips, and the man who has called the twelve will also call the fifty. Then in the last round I may check, I may tap—it all depends upon the number of chips left to bet and the character of the man who has stayed with me.

Third- and Fourth-Round Betting

Here is where you have to shift for yourself. If you happen to have an "immortal" at this point, you want to build the pot up as high as possible, and whether this is best accomplished by means of checking, making a small bet or making a large bet depends upon too many considerations to be discussed in a book. Conversely, if your opponent has a possible "immortal" against you, it is up to you to figure out whether or not he has this hand. However, there is one very important consideration in these last rounds, namely: the number of chips in front of you and the other players. If you have a great many chips beware of the possible "immortal." If you have only a few chips remember the "immortal" can take these chips and no more, and hence does not present as much potential danger.

Playing a Small Pair

With a small pair back to back it is unwise to raise on an early round of the betting, the reason being that any other player is likely to have a higher pair and raise you back. Now if you call you are hooked for all your chips. In fact it is pretty good policy never to raise at all with a small pair, but if you must raise wait until the fifth card. Then if no one shows strength and you feel pretty confident that there is not an "immortal" out against you, you may, if you desire, take a chance and bet in the hope of getting a call.

Limit Stud

The essential difference between Limit Stud and Table Stakes lies in the fact that in Table Stakes your principal aim is either to win the very big pots or not to be in them; whereas in Limit Stud there are no very big pots, and your aim is to build up the pot any time you think you may have the best hand, even though someone may actually have you beaten.

Furthermore, in Limit Stud there is little percentage, if any, in wasting chips for advertising purposes. Thus if you are the high man in a Limit game, with something like a jack or a ten, and have a deuce or three in the hole, you might just as well turn your hand without betting. If you show an ace or a king, however, you should always open on the chance that everyone will drop.

Initial Raise

In a Limit game if you happen to hold a small pair back to back or an ace or king in the hole, and are one of the last players to act, you should raise. True, you may be betting into a higher pair, but nevertheless the chances favor your having the best two-card hand, and accordingly you should start to build up a large pot.

Later Betting

The later betting is, of course, based on your observation of the relative strength and weakness shown by the different players and by the amount of money already in the pot. While it is not particularly good tactics to bet into a possible "immortal," the amount that such a procedure can cost you is nowhere near so great as it might be in a Table Stakes game. Hence, any time you think you have the best hand, go ahead and bet.

Stud Poker with the Four Flush

While ordinary Stud is the tightest of all poker games, it is possible to transform it into one of the finest and most liberal by a couple of simple steps. First we introduce a new poker hand—the four flush (i.e., four cards of one suit and one card of another suit). This hand ranks above one pair but below two pairs.

The second step consists of introducing a large ante and a limit which increases with each round of betting.[1] I would suggest one of the two following scales:

Scale A—Ante: Two chips per player.
     Limit: First round—one chip.
        Second round—two chips.
        Third round—three chips.
        Last round—five chips.

[1] Of course the four flush can be introduced into any Stud game without changing either the ante or the limit.

If any player shows a pair, the limit is immediately five chips.

Scale B—Ante: One chip per player.
Limit: First, second and third rounds
—one chip.
Last round, or any pair shown
—two chips.

Either of these scales gives everyone plenty of excuse to stay, so that practically the only time a player drops out is when he has two very low cards in different suits.

Now, since people are playing liberally, anybody with an ace or king in the hole or a pair back to back is going to raise on the first card. As a result, by the time the later cards are dealt there is so much money in the pot that no one who sees any possible chance of winning is going to drop out, while the players who have a good chance are going to raise back and forth.

The only real technique in this game consists of pushing good hands to the limit. For instance, if you have a pair back to back, raise on the first card, and if you are raised back, raise again. True, the man who has raised back may have a better pair than you, but you are undoubtedly better than the other four or five players who are trailing along and hence are getting very good odds for your money.

Furthermore, if your first three cards are of the same suit, the chances are only three to two against your making a four flush. Accordingly, if there are several people in the pot it is well worth your while to raise several times, unless there is a pair showing. You may be certain that the player who is raising you back has already made a pair, but the odds are greatly against his improving further. Hence there is a definite percentage in favor of your raising back.

Another situation where you can afford to raise on possibilities occurs when your first four cards consist of, say, the queen, ten, deuce of spades and another deuce. In this situation ten cards will give you a four flush, six cards two pairs and two cards three of a kind. In other words, you have eighteen chances out of forty-eight of improving, and the odds against you are but five to three. Accordingly, with several people in the pot, you should raise against a better hand purely on possibilities.

Limit of Raises

Suppose on the third card Player A has an ace in the hole and shows an ace and deuce, while Player B has the jack of spades in the hole and shows the ten and nine of the same suit, and there are several other players in the pot with low pairs already made. Player A has the best hand and obviously is going to be willing to keep on raising as long as anyone else will. Player B, on the other hand, knows the odds are but three to two against his making a four flush and furthermore that he has some slight extra chance of making a straight or even a five-card flush. Accordingly, if he is a real gambling player he may keep on raising indefinitely also. Meanwhile the other players who have started in the pot will trail along indefinitely, hoping against hope that each raise will be the last. Therefore, in order to prevent this situation, the number of raises on any particular round of betting should be limited to four or five.

Stakes

In playing this game the winnings and losings are likely to be about five times as great as in a regular Stud game for the same stakes. Accordingly, in playing it for the first time, you should either cut your stakes down or prepare in advance to settle for not more than twenty to twenty-five cents on the dollar.

Down-the-River (Seven-Card Stud)

The fascination of this game lies in the fact that since each player shows four cards you can formulate a pretty good idea as to what each of your opponents probably has. At the same time the three concealed cards may all be of the same denomination as one he shows, thereby giving him four of a kind with nothing at all showing.

In the early rounds of betting the novice is apt to want to follow the old Stud rule of staying whenever he can beat anything showing. This is bad since, as each player has two cards in the hole, the chances are very strong that one player at least will have something extra to start with. Accordingly, you should stay on the first card only if you have a pair or three cards to a flush or three in succession.

If you happen to hold a pair, it is decidedly more

advantageous to have both cards of the pair concealed than to have one showing. For example, you show a five and have a pair of nines in the hole. If you draw another nine you have three nines, and no one is likely to suspect it. On the other hand, if you start with a nine up and a nine and five in the hole and catch another nine, you will have two of them showing.

If the fourth card does not improve your hand in any way, bear in mind that the other players may have improved. Accordingly, if a bet is made and all you have is a low pair, you will be well advised to drop.

On the fifth card, unless you hold a very high pair or have a four flush or an open-end straight, you should surely get out if anyone bets.

On the sixth card you should have a pretty good idea from the cards showing and the betting as to what the other players hold. Furthermore, you are now at the real danger point of the hand. For instance, suppose you have two pairs. If you call here you are practically committed to call also on the final round. Incidentally, this two-pair hand is the great come-on in this game since, while it is a decidedly better than average hand, it is very seldom that it will win a big pot.

If on the sixth card you have a four flush or an open-end straight, there is nearly always enough money in the pot so that the mathematics favor your calling any bet that is made. However, before calling on possibilities, look over the other hands carefully and make sure that there is a very good chance that you will win the pot if you are fortunate enough to make your hand. Here is an example:

Your first six cards are an ace, a pair of eights, a seven, a six and a five, with no possibility of making a flush. Player A shows a jack, a ten and a nine. Player B shows three spades. Both A and B have been betting and now one of them bets. Even though you have already put a lot of money in the pot, it is a very good idea to drop out because the best you can make is a nine-high straight, and from the cards you see there is a strong probability that Player A holds a higher straight or that Player B already has his flush, in which event you have no chance to win the pot at all.

In this game, since most players stay for a fourth card and many stay for a fifth, there are a great many cards exposed and it is particularly important to keep track of all these cards. First, they give you a clue to the possibilities of your own hand. For example, four of your first five cards are spades and only one other spade has appeared anywhere on the table. This means there are eight spades unaccounted for and your chance of getting one on the next two rounds is quite good. However, if in addition to your four spades five others have appeared, there are but four spades unaccounted for and your chance of making a flush is only half what it was in the other instance.

If you have a pair of tens and no other ten appears, you have a right to keep on hoping to draw a third. But once a ten appears anywhere else on the table, your chance of making a third is promptly cut in half.

The cards that appear also give you a good clue as to what your opponents may have. Thus if someone shows a pair of tens and you are able to account for both the other tens, you know he cannot have one in the hole. Or if he shows four spades and you can account for all nine other spades, you do not have to fear a flush. However, if he shows a pair of tens and you are able to account for only one other ten, remember there is really an excellent chance that he has the fourth ten in the hole. Otherwise he will be likely to drop out.

Or let us consider this instance: The first two cards Player A shows are both hearts. He bets out strongly. On the next round several hearts appear, but he draws a spade and now merely calls. On the following round he draws another heart and again bets out very strongly. In looking around the table and at your hole cards you are now able to account for eight hearts in addition to the three that he shows. Accordingly, in order for him to have a flush, he must have the only two missing hearts in the hole. As a matter of mathematics this is a very remote possibility. On the other hand, you might say to yourself: "He sees all these other hearts also; hence, if he doesn't have his flush already made, why is he betting so strongly?"

Stakes

Since there are five rounds of betting in this game, it should be borne in mind that the number of chips won or lost will be approximately twice as great as in a straight Stud game with the same limit.

High-Low Five-Card Stud

If ever there was a dynamite game, this is it. You start with a pair of aces back to back. Another man going for low gets a pair on the fourth card and a second pair on the fifth card to win high from you. Or your first four cards are a two, three, four and seven. You bet boldly, only to get a second deuce on the last card. Now someone with a king and a jack in his hand beats you out for low.

Accordingly, since anything can happen, the average player makes a habit of always staying for a third card. Then he is encouraged to take a fourth card, and finally, when the last round of betting starts, he is likely to find himself so deeply in the pot he must go through to the end.

Unlike most High-Low games, where the proper tactics are to play for low, in this game the best start is a high pair back to back. The reason for this is that, no matter how good your hand may look for low, you can be ruined if the last card pairs you. On the other hand, if you start out for high, your hand can get no worse.

Unlike other High-Low games, the possibilities for real bluffs in this game are tremendous. Naturally the big money is won when one player gets an "immortal" high, another gets an "immortal" low, and nevertheless one or more other players stay through to the finish. In order to build up those desirable situations it is essential that a player maintain some reputation for bluffing. For instance, consider the following situation:

On the fourth card Player A shows a pair of aces. Players B, C and D are obviously playing for low. Player B shows an eight, seven and four, turns up a deuce and takes his last card down.[2] Players C and D, who show a nine and ten respectively, also take their last cards down. Accordingly, Player A has a sure thing for high, while if Player B has been lucky enough to draw a six, a five or a three, he has a sure thing for low.

Player A bets. Player B raises. Now if C and D both know that B never bluffs, they drop out. On the other hand, if B is accustomed to bluffing, both C and D say to themselves: "Maybe B has been unlucky enough to draw a second eight, in which case we have him beaten for low." Now either C or D is going to make up his mind to go through.

As a converse to the bluff, a player may trail along with an "immortal," hoping to encourage someone else to bet his hand for him. Take the same situation. Player B makes his "immortal" but merely calls A's bet. Now C, who has made a nine low, decides that B has drawn a jack or a queen and raises. A raises back. B merely calls and C raises again.

Of course that particular type of betting by C doesn't happen often, and in fact the rule of straight Stud: "Do not bet against a possible

[2]See Law 5—High-Low.

'immortal' when you can be raised back," applies with greater force, if anything, in this game than at straight Stud.

When a player with three low cards showing decides to take his last card face up there is a strong presumption that he either has a small pair or a high card in the hole, since with a low card in the hole he would probably take his last card down, thereby concealing his hand from his opponents. However, it is very good tactics on occasion to take your last card up even though this is not the case. Now the other players, who do not have as good lows as you, are likely to decide that you are really going for high.

The following hand, taken from a Table Stakes game in which I played several years ago, is a good example of deception: On the first card Player A, sitting immediately to my left, showed an ace and opened. Player B stayed. I raised with a deuce. A and B both called. On the third card it was checked around to me. I bet. Player A stayed; Player B raised; I called. On the fourth round A checked. B bet right out and I called.

At this point the situation was as follows: I showed a six, a four and a two and had an eight-spot in the hole. Accordingly, I turned up the eight-spot and took my next card down. To my disgust it was an ace. Player B, showing the ace, six and four, took his last card up and drew a ten. Player C, who showed a jack, a nine and a five, took his last card up and got a three.

Player A checked. Player B made a moderate

bet and I raised him exactly one chip. Player A called. Player B made a substantial raise. I called. Player A raised one chip and Player B tapped. I called and Player A called.

Player A had aces back to back and won high. Player B, with jacks back to back, was in the middle and immediately said to me, "How could you dare call me when I tapped? When A raised one chip he finally gave away the fact that he had his aces back to back. At the same time your betting had clearly shown that your last card had ruined your low hand. Therefore you should have reasoned that my tap was based on a low hand plus the knowledge of the fact that your last card had hurt you."

I replied: "My call was based on an entirely different type of reasoning. First, I decided that your early bet indicated jacks back to back, though of course you might have been trying to give that very impression with a low card in the hole. However, let us consider the last round of betting. You bet right out and I raised one chip only. Now with aces back to back, an ordinary player in A's position would have raised, figuring that he and I had you in the middle. But A made a better play by merely calling my bet. At this point there was no way you could tell that I didn't have a sure thing for low. Hence your second raise definitely confirmed the fact that you had a jack in the hole. At the same time I know Player A pretty well, and when he stayed for your bet and my one-chip raise I decided he had aces back to back. Accordingly, when you bet I merely called your raise, feeling certain that A would raise back. Now when A did raise one chip you finally knew that he had aces. But at this point you had so much money in the pot you decided on one last desperate effort—a tap —in the hope that I would drop out. But since I already had marked you with jacks, my call was just as sure as if I really had an 'immortal.'"

Since the rules of this game allow a player the option of turning up his hole card and taking his fifth card face down, there is a great opportunity for maneuvering in that connection. For instance, suppose you show an eight, six and five and have a deuce in the hole and every other player shows a nine or higher card. You turn up your deuce, take your last card face down and now, if you draw a three, a four or a seven, you have an absolute "immortal" for low against the rest of the game. On the other hand, if you draw a second eight you can still bet just as if you had an "immortal" and you are at least in an excellent position to have your bluff succeed.

Accordingly, in this situation the average player automatically asks for his last card face down. Hence, when he fails to do so, there is a strong presumption that his hole card is either a very high one or pairs one of the small cards he shows, and that actually he hopes to win the high half of the pot—not the low half.

And now here is where the real expert in a Table Stakes game occasionally builds up a big pot. Even though he has a deuce in the hole, he takes his last card up. Now if he draws a three, the other players are very unlikely to suspect that he has an "immortal" low, since if he had it he would normally have taken his last card down. Therefore he stands a very good chance of collecting all of someone's chips.

On the other side of the picture there is the case of the player who shows a small pair. Now if his other card gives him either three of a kind or a second pair, he naturally is not going to turn it up; whereas if it doesn't help him, he will turn it up so that if the fifth card helps him his hand will be concealed. But the winning player should reverse this situation on occasion and, even though his hole card does not help his pair, take his last card up.

High-Low Seven-Card Stud

General Principles

The first and by far the most important principle of this game is: Play for low. The reason for this lies in the fact that if you start with low cards you always have a chance of winding up with a straight or a flush or some other combination of cards which will win high; while at the same time your low cards will give you low and you may win the entire pot. Starting with high cards, you may win high, but it is practically impossible ever to win low.

Of course most people will say to themselves: "If there are several people in the pot trying for low and I am the only one trying for high, I obviously have a better chance to win high than anyone else, and half the pot will then show me a good profit. Why doesn't the percentage favor my playing with a holding such as two kings and a queen?"

The answer to this is that, if all players who start in the pot were automatically committed to play until the finish, it would be a good percentage to play for high. Actually what happens is that a player who starts with a high pair almost always stays right through to the end, whereas the players with low cards drop out as soon as they see that some other hand is developing better than theirs. For instance, consider a hypothetical case in a Table Stakes game:

A starts with high cards and B, C, D and E start with low cards. Each player has one hundred and fifty chips in front of him and bets one chip on the first round, putting five chips in the pot. The second-round bet is four chips, but Player E, who does not like his fourth card, drops out. Now there are twenty-one chips in the pot. The third-round bet is twenty chips, and Player D does not bother to call that. This puts eighty-one chips in the pot and each player in the pot has one hundred and twenty-five chips left. On the sixth card either B or C taps. A stays more or less automatically (once you start with high cards you nearly always feel obligated to go right on through) and the other player drops. There are now three hundred and thirty-one chips in the pot. If A's high hand stands up, he collects one hundred and sixty-six and thereby shows a clear profit of sixteen chips. If his hand fails to stand up, he has lost one hundred and fifty.

Now suppose the other low hand stays for the tap. There will be four hundred and fifty-six chips in the pot, one half of which will be two hundred and twenty-eight. A's profit, if he should win high, will be seventy-eight chips, or slightly more than a fifty-per-cent return on the amount he risked. That still looks like a pretty good return if it weren't for one thing—that when Player B bet the hundred and twenty-five chips Player C's call would very likely be predicated on the fact that his low cards had shaped up to give him a flush or a straight. And so, when the two low players stay to the finish, the chance that A's two pairs or one high pair will win high is not too good.

In a Limit game the percentage against the player who starts with high cards is by no means so great, since proportionately more chips are bet on the first rounds than in the latter stages. Nevertheless, this percentage is there, and the player who likes to start out with high cards is an *absolutely sure loser*[3] in any Seven-Card High-Low game.

In this game, more than any other, a player must constantly bear in mind the fact that once he puts chips in the pot they are not his any more; and if

---

[3] I once was discussing the technique of three players who lost continually in this game because of their propensity for playing high hands. My remark was, "It's a pleasure to have Smith in the game. He's always in there calling on two pairs. Jones is even better. He's in there calling with one pair. But Brown is best of all—he'll call you with an ace and a king."

you keep getting cards which do not help your hand, while other players' cards appear to be of value, you had better get out immediately. As an example, suppose your first three cards are the seven, four and two of spades—about as good a holding as you could wish to have—and you probably raise on the first card. Now you get the king of diamonds and, while your ardor is somewhat cooled, you nevertheless stay for a fifth card, which turns out to be the queen of clubs. At this point a great many players, merely out of a feeling of annoyance, will stay for a sixth card. Staying in this situation is distinctly a losing proposition. If the sixth card is no good, you have merely wasted the chips you paid to draw it; while even if the sixth card is a good one and helps your hand, the odds are greatly against the seventh card also being what you want.

If on the sixth card you have made a low hand, which obviously is better than anything anyone else can have at that time, you should bet right out in order to make anyone who wishes to outdraw you pay for that privilege. I can remember once violating this rule myself with disastrous results. It was late in the evening. The game was Table Stakes, and one other player and myself each had a great many chips in front of us. My first six cards were an eight, seven, six, five, four, three, giving me an eight-high straight and an eight, six, five, four, three for low. My opponent showed the ace and deuce of diamonds, the king of spades and the seven of hearts.

The pot was not particularly big, and I foolishly bet a mere one third of my chips, which bet was promptly called. My opponent and I each received our last card, and my opponent tapped me. I realized this tap indicated one of three things: (a) he had made a flush; (b) he had made a seven low; (c) he had caught a pigeon[4] and made both of them. In case of (a) or (b) I would divide the pot, and I would lose both ways only in event (c). Accordingly, I called and, unfortunately for me, his pigeon had flown in and his hole cards were the six, four and three of diamonds. I lost all my chips. However, if I had tapped on the sixth card, this player probably could not have afforded to call on mere possibilities.

When you stay for a sixth-card bet on possibilities you should endeavor to be reasonably certain that if you do make your hand you will win the pot. For example, don't stay in an effort to make a straight when there is a good chance that someone else will have a flush. Or don't try for an eight low when someone else possibly already has a seven low.

Valuing Hands

The beginner in this game is likely to be confused in counting the possibilities of his own and his

---

[4] The word "pigeon" has recently been included in our poker vocabulary and means any particularly valuable card that you get. In particular, in the Seven-Card game it means a last card which wins both ways for the player who is lucky enough to draw it. Thus in this instance his pigeon was a low diamond.

opponents' hands. In this connection the following
table will prove of help:

1. The best low hand a player with a full house
can make is a pair.

2. The best low hand a player with three of a
kind or two pairs can make is represented by the
highest card in his hand.

3. A player with a straight or flush must use
one card outside that straight or flush in his low
hand.

Immortals

"Immortals" occur with great frequency in this
game. In particular the lowest hand your opponent
can have is represented by the two lowest cards he
shows combined with three other concealed cards.
As an example, if your opponent shows a ten, nine,
eight, seven, his best possible low will be an eight,
seven, four, three, two. Now if your low hand is an
eight, six, five, four, three, you must win low from
him.

Another and very important type of "immortal"
occurs when a player's hand is such that he is certain he will win either high or low from his opponent. For example, your seven cards are a jack, a
pair of nines, a seven, four, three and two—not a
very good hand. But your opponent shows the
queen of spades, the eight of hearts, the eight of
diamonds and the deuce of clubs. If he has three
low cards in the hole he will have an eight low and
beat your low hand, but in that event your pair of
nines will win high. On the other hand, if he has

two pairs, three of a kind or a straight, he will beat you for high but you will win low.

When holding an "immortal" on the last card, get in the habit of betting the limit. As an example, suppose you have an "immortal" low and nothing at all for high. The only other player shows a pair of kings. He doesn't know that you have nothing for high, and if you bet the limit against him, he may decide to drop. Even if he calls, you have lost nothing since you still get back half the pot.

Staying on the First Card

The only high holdings worth staying on are (a) three of a kind, and (b) three cards to a flush; although if you want to play liberally, you might occasionally stay for one round with a pair of aces or kings or three cards in sequence.

Any three cards, eight-spot or lower, are worth staying on since all three are good cards for low. A nine is only a fair card, and I would not stay with a nine, eight and deuce although I would with a nine, seven and deuce.

When you get up to the ten-spot or higher, you have a card which is practically useless, and I stay only if both my low cards are below the seven.

If you have a pair, remember that one card in that pair is absolutely useless for low and might as well not be in your hand at all.

With borderline holdings, the fact that you have two cards in the same suit or that your three cards all might fit as part of a straight gives you a slight additional percentage for high and may allow you to stay. Thus a nine, eight, seven is a pretty good hand on which to stay since you have distinct possibilities for both high and low.

If a player with a low card raises on the first round, it is good policy to get out unless your hand is pretty good since the probabilities are that this player has three perfect or nearly perfect cards.

Second-Round Betting

Here your procedure is determined by what you start with and what you and the other players drew. For instance, if you started with a low card showing and drew another low card, so that on the surface your hand appears better than any other, in a Table Stakes game you should bet irrespective of your hole cards. Otherwise the other players would know that when you did bet in that situation you also had two good cards in the hole.

In a Limit game, however, you might check on occasion. As a matter of fact, the very finest players sometimes check in a Table Stakes game in a situation such as the following: They start with a five and two in the hole and a three up and now get a four. No one else looks very good on the surface, and they are afraid that if they bet right out everyone will drop. Accordingly, they check in order to simulate weakness.

If you start with three perfect cards and now get a face card, you may still afford to stay unless a player showing two perfect cards indicates great strength; while if everyone else gets a bad card, you can even afford to bet right out.

If you start with one bad card and happen to get
a second one, drop immediately. Even though
every other player shows at least one bad card, it
is a cinch that someone has two good cards in the
hole. Now in order for you to have anything you
must get three good cards out of three, while all
he needs is two out of three, and hence the percentage in his favor is too much to play against.

Third-Round Betting

The third round, or fifth card, is the key point
of the hand. In a Table Stakes game the first large
bets usually are made, while in a Limit game the
player who stays for third-round bet will usually go
through to the finish. Accordingly, it is right at this
point that you had better get out, unless it appears
that your chances are as good as or better than
those of anyone else. In determining your chances
you must consider possibilities for both high and
low. For instance, your first five cards are an eight,
a six, a three and a pair of deuces. Another player
shows a pair of eights and a three. You really have
a pretty good hand, but if the other player has two
perfect cards in the hole his chance for low is just
about as good as yours, while if neither of you improves for high or each of you improves in an equal
amount, since his pair of eights is better than your
twos, he will beat you for high anyway. Accordingly, you are at a distinct disadvantage as against
that one player, and we might give the following
rule which applies at all times: *If you have a pair,
beware of the player who shows a higher pair.*

Let us consider another instance. You have the same five cards. Another player shows the seven and three of spades and the four of hearts and now makes a large bet. Before calling that large bet you might well say to yourself, "This player either has a straight or a low hand already made. All I have is a chance for an eight low and very few possibilities for high against anything good. Why should I pay a lot of chips to see if I can improve my hand?"

Fourth-Round Betting

Your sixth-card procedure has already been discussed in General Principles. If you have a hand already made, which is going to stand up irrespective of what the other players get for their seventh cards, you can afford to make a small bet. But if they can draw out on you, you had best make it as large as possible in order to make them pay for staying.

Conversely, if you have possibilities but nothing made, make sure that you are drawing to something that ought to win the pot, not merely cost you chips on the last round.

Last-Round Betting

Troubles in this Seven-Card High-Low game are cumulative. A bad stay on the first round leaves you a second-round problem. Liberal second-round play results in a third-round headache. Now if you put in chips on the third round you may expect more annoyance on the fourth. Finally, if you stay to draw the last card, by this time you have usually put so many chips in the pot that you now must call the last-round bet.

Accordingly, the best advice I can give for last-round betting is: Be sure your first six cards are good enough so that when the last-round betting takes place your opponents will be calling you—not you them.

The Player with Few Chips

In a Table Stakes game it frequently happens that one or two players have very few chips in comparison with the rest, and the presence of these players creates a distinct problem. First, if a player with few chips stays in the pot he is likely to bet all of them at an early stage on the theory that several people who have a lot of chips will call this small bet. Then later on, in betting against one another, some of the players with a great many chips will be driven out, so the player with few chips is getting a good percentage proposition.

The rules for the division of side money provide that if a player with no interest in the side money wins one way and a player interested in the side money wins the other, then that player takes all the side money. Accordingly, if you become involved in the pot with one player with a lot of chips and another player with few chips, beware of the situation where obviously the player with but few chips is trying to win the same half of the pot as you. The reason is that if you beat him, all you get back of the side money is your own share, and your profit is represented merely by one half of his few chips. But if he beats you, the third player takes all the side money and you have lost all your chips.

Position Play

Particularly on the last round your position at the table is of great importance in determining your course of action. For instance, a bet is made and you have a doubtful call. If there is anyone back of you who is likely to raise, it is pretty good policy to drop. Conversely, if there is no one in back of you, you can afford to call.

Two-Handed Play

If at any stage of the game you are left in the pot with one other player always endeavor to build up a situation where you have a cinch for one way. Once you have attained this position, you can tap in a Table Stakes game or bet the limit in a Limit game. Now if he calls, you get your money back; while he may fail to call for fear that you can win both ways.

Conversely, when you realize that the other player has a cinch for one way against you it is advisable to get out unless the amount of money already in the pot warrants your risking the additional amount you may be forced to bet. The following examples will show how you act:

Example 1. It is a Table Stakes game. Your first four cards are three kings and a six, while the only other player in the pot shows the seven and six of spades. There are fifty chips in the pot and each of you has over a thousand left. He bets the size of the pot. You should drop, the reason for this being that if you don't drop he will bet more and more until finally all your chips are in. Then if you do win high your gain is but twenty-five chips, represented by half the pot before it became two handed. But if you don't win high (and there is a good chance that he will come out with a straight or a flush and that you won't make your full house), then you have lost over a thousand.

However, suppose it is down to the last card and you are the last man to act. There are about fifteen hundred chips in the pot, and a player showing the king, three and deuce of diamonds and seven of hearts taps. Everyone drops until it comes to your turn, and you find you have but two hundred chips left.

Here the percentage favors calling with even a pair of jacks, since if you do win one way, your gain is almost four times what you have risked.

Bluffing

Bluffs in this game fall into two general forms: (1) the bet by a player who looks as if he has low but actually has bad cards in the hole, designed to drive out the other low players; (2) the bluff by the player who looks as if he has a good high hand but actually has only a fair high hand, designed to drive out the other high players.

The great weakness of both these bluffs lies in the fact that the player who now calls you because he imagines he can win the other half of the pot actually wins the whole pot.

Concealment

On the last card it is frequently necessary to conceal your hand by refusing to bet or raise. For instance, you are obviously going for high and actually have a full house. The player to your left also is going for high, while the man to your right has what looks like a sure thing for low. It is your first bet but you check. The other high hand checks also. Now the low player bets. All you can afford to do is to call since a raise would surely drive the third player out.

Ace High and Low

A great many people like to play this game with the ace counted both as high and low. This variation does not affect the game materially except that players must bear in mind that once the ace is counted as a low card, the value of all other cards is lessened. Thus a nine-spot, instead of being a fair card, becomes a bad card; the eight, instead of being a good card, becomes a fair card; and the seven, instead of being a very good card, is merely a good card. The only card which improves any is the six since it is now a part of the perfect low hand.

Furthermore, the ace becomes of particular importance since not only is it the lowest card, but also it may frequently turn out that a player starting with an ace will wind up winning high with aces up or even a pair of aces.

For instance, suppose there are two players in the pot in a Table Stakes Seven-Card game. If there is no declaration, the one with an "immortal" low taps and now the other player, with two pairs, may be afraid to call because the low man may also have a straight or a flush. The same danger applies in a declaring game but by no means in so great a manner. Thus, suppose Player A's seven cards are a ten, an eight, a six, a five, a four, a three and a deuce. He has an eight for low and a straight for high. He taps. Player B calls, showing a king, a queen and a pair of nines. Actually the pair of nines is all he has for high. In all probability Player A will be afraid to declare both high and low since if he does that, and Player B holds either a straight or a full house, Player B will then win the entire pot. Hence Player A merely declares low. Player B declares high and gets half the pot automatically.

When players declare in order, starting with the last one to bet or raise, there is considerable jockeying for position since, obviously, the last player to announce has a great advantage. However, this leads to some very fine bluffing situations. For example, in a five-card game a player appears to have an "immortal" low but actually has a pair. He now bets out strongly and promptly announces low, whereupon in all likelihood all the other players remaining in the pot will declare high.

When the players declare simultaneously by means of chips there is no need for this jockeying for position. However, when it gets down to but two players the one who calls with a doubtful hand must be ready for a surprise. For instance, suppose you show a king, seven, six and two and have an ace in the hole in a five-card game. Another player showing an eight, five, four and three bets. Everyone drops and you call. Naturally you assume that when he opens his hand he will show a white chip, indicating low. However, it turns out he had a pair of eights back to back all the time. Both of you declare for high and he wins all the pot.

Conclusion

I have devoted a great deal of space to this particular game because, once played, it invariably becomes about the most popular game there is. But the beginner had better proceed cautiously because this is a complicated game and even today I frequently encounter new problems.

Declaring High-Low

In this variation the fact that it is necessary for each player to declare whether he is trying for high, for low or for both does not materially affect the conditions which warrant a player staying in the pot, raising, etc. However, it does affect the later stages of the betting.

CHAPTER VII

Various Other Games

Dealer's Option

A GREAT MANY POKER PLAYERS become bored if one game is played all evening. As a result Dealer's Option, in which the dealer has the right to name the conditions of play, has acquired great popularity. In playing Dealer's Option the following points should be kept in mind:

1. The dealer's option should be restricted to not more than seven or eight games. Otherwise the players simply vie with one another in seeing what absurdities they can concoct.

In playing Dealer's Option you should beware of this. For instance, I know one man who claimed he had a sure-fire system of winning in that game. When asked what it was he explained, "Whenever I deal, I deal a hand of straight Draw Poker with the deuces, threes and fours wild and the further provision that the high hand and the dealer split the pot!"

2. Every time a new game is played it has the same effect as an increase in stakes, the reason being that at first the players have a distinct ten-

dency to overvalue their hands and hence bet more, proportionately, than they would in a familiar game.

3. The factor of skill is increased and the element of luck decreased. A lot of people are going to disagree with this statement, but there is a distinct reason for it. If only one or two games are played, after a while even the poorest players obtain a pretty good idea of what a hand is worth and how to play it. But when each deal presents something entirely new it takes an expert to know what is going on.

The following games all possess distinct merit and are well worth trying.

Spit-in-the-Ocean

Each player is dealt four cards and one card is faced up in the center. This card and all like it are wild and it is counted as part of your hand. Otherwise the conditions of the game are the same as in Draw, and after a round of betting the players draw to their hands and bet again.

In playing this game you should bear in mind that every player starts with one joker and that there are three more jokers in the deck. If you haven't got them, someone else almost surely has. As a result, nothing less than four of a kind is likely to win any pot, and even a small straight flush is nothing to get too excited about although it is a fairly good hand.

There is no point whatsoever in staying with a

pat straight or flush, much less trying to make one. In deciding whether to stay, a joker in your hand is much more valuable than a pair. I would suggest the following minimum requirements for staying in the pot: (a) a joker; (b) a pair of aces or kings; (c) two pairs, jacks up or better.

With the last hand, if there is a raise before the draw, either drop out or discard your small pair since your full house is not going to win the pot.

Spit-in-the-Ocean is also frequently played with three cards in the center and four in each player's hand. The cards are turned up one at a time, each exposure being followed by a round of betting, after which there is a draw and a final round. In this game, even though no cards are wild, you should not expect ever to win a pot with less than a high flush.

Cincinnati

In this game there are five cards in your hand and five in the center. Nothing is wild and there is no draw, but there are five rounds of betting, one round following the turning up of each of the center cards. A straight may win a pot and a big flush has about an even chance of standing up.

If as many as three cards in one suit turn up it is almost a certainty that some player will have a flush, while if a pair turns up someone is pretty sure to have a full house. As a matter of fact, even without a pair turning up, full houses occur with considerable frequency. On the other hand, any four of a kind is a very good hand and will win more than nine pots out of ten.

Cincinnati Liz

In this variation of Cincinnati the lowest card in the center and all like it are wild.

Practically the smallest hand that ever wins a pot is a large four of a kind. Straight flushes stand up on occasion, but the only really good hand is five aces.

High-Low Cincinnati

This is really a fine game. With five cards in the center and five cards in the hand there is plenty of opportunity for a player to win a pot both ways. Furthermore, in the event that two or three low cards show up in the center, it is not at all uncommon to find that two players tie for low.

Assuming the betting starts before a card is faced up, I stay if: (a) I have three cards that fit into the perfect low, or any four fairly low cards (this hand presents distinct possibilities for low); (b) I have a pair of aces, two pairs, a four flush or three cards of the same suit including an ace (these hands present possibilities for high); (c) I have a holding which suggests possibilities for either high or low, such as a fairly high pair and three low cards.

I pay no attention whatsoever to straights since, even if made, the chances are greatly against my straight winning high.

My subsequent procedure is now based on how the cards that appear in the center match my hand. Thus, if I am playing for low and a high card appears in the center, I say to myself, "Here is one card that did no one any good as regards my half of the pot." If a low card turns up which happens to pair one of my own, I say, "This did me no good at all but surely helped someone else," and I am inclined to get right out unless my hand already is very good; while if a low card that helps my hand appears, I am greatly encouraged.

If I am trying for high, with a holding such as a pair of aces, and if the first card doesn't happen to be either a third ace or a pair for one of my cards, I am inclined to get out, the reason being that I still need two cards to make my full house and must get those two out of the four cards remaining.

If I happen to have a small full house and a pair higher in value than my set of threes appears in the center, I realize the distinct likelihood that that gives someone else a higher full house and either drop out or at least stop raising.

If I have a small flush and three cards in some other suit appear in the center, I am likewise discouraged. In fact two cards of another suit act as a distinct warning to me.

Finally, I try to pay attention to the betting. In particular, if one or two players show great strength in the early rounds, I realize that the eventual winning hands will have to be pretty good and drop out unless I have possibilities of making something very good. On the other hand, when no one shows strength I will trail along with only fair possibilities.

Six-Card Stud

There are two ways of playing this game. First, each player starts with two hole cards and one up card and eventually gets three more up cards. Hence there are three rounds of betting and considerable opportunity for deception.

In staying in the early rounds, all you have to do is follow the same principles as you would in Seven-Card Stud, except that potential straights and flushes are considerably less valuable than in that game and high pairs considerably better.

In the other variation each player starts with one hole card only, and one up card and the last card is dealt face down, thereby giving five rounds of betting. This variation of the game is not so satisfactory as the other one.

Six-Card Stud, High-Low Divide

In this game, unlike straight Six-Card Stud, the more interesting variation occurs when the player gets his sixth card down. As in Five-Card High-Low, the best start is a high pair back to back. One high card and one low card are worth practically nothing, particularly if the high card is exposed; while two low cards are always a good stay. Furthermore, if no one shows great signs of a straight or a flush, three of a kind becomes a terrific hand and two pairs a good hand.

When each player starts with two hole cards and one up card the best start is three of a kind, and the next best start three very low cards.

Shotgun

I imagine this game, which is a cross between Draw and Stud, derives its name from the fact that the beginner has less chance to escape with his whole skin than at most any other game. The rules are as follows:

Each player is dealt three cards, and following a round of betting those remaining in the pot receive a fourth card. Then there is a second round of betting; a fifth card is dealt, followed by a third round of betting and a draw. Following the draw there is a fourth and final round of betting.

Like all games with several rounds of betting, the first thing to learn is to drop out on the first card if you have nothing. In particular I would recommend dropping unless you have either a pair or three cards of the same suit. If you want to waste a few chips you may also stay on three cards in sequence, but this latter is not recommended.

If after receiving the fourth card someone bets, you should drop unless you have a fair-sized pair, a four flush or an open-end straight. After getting a fifth card you should value your hand about the same as you would in Draw Poker, except that you must modify your valuation to allow for the way the betting has gone.

Incidentally, in this game, for simplicity's sake, it is customary for the player nearest the dealer's left to bet first on every round. This, of course, makes the dealer the last man and gives him a slight advantage.

Double-Barreled Shotgun
(Sometimes called Texas Tech)

This game is simply Shotgun plus two additional features. First, the high and the low hands divide; second, there are four rounds of betting after the draw instead of one, these four rounds occurring as follows:

After the draw each player exposes one card. There is a round of betting. A second card is exposed and there is a second round of betting. A third card is exposed, followed by a third round of betting. Finally a fourth card is exposed, followed by the final round. The order of betting is the same as in Stud (i.e., the player who shows the highest card or cards on the table bets first).

Following the last round of betting each player remaining in the pot places a chip in his hand—one color meaning he is trying for high, another color meaning he is trying for low. The hands then open simultaneously.

The division of the pot is now accomplished as follows: The highest hand of all those declaring for high wins high; the lowest hand of all those declaring for low wins low. Thus, if only one player declares for high, he wins that half of the pot even though he may not actually have the highest hand.

Frequently there is a great deal of skill involved in deciding which way to declare in this game. As an example, you're in the pot with but one opponent. You show a two, a three, a four and a seven and have a seven concealed. He shows a two, a five, an eight and a jack. You have been betting very strongly, and your opponent is going to assume that you have an "immortal" low against him. Hence, irrespective of what his hole card is, he will declare for high. Therefore, if you want to play safe you may declare for low and be perfectly sure of splitting the pot. However, if you want to gamble you may declare high. Now unless he has an eight or jack in the hole you will win the entire pot. However, if he does have an eight or a jack in the hole, you will lose it all.

Pistol or Hole-Card Stud

In this game of Five-Card Stud the betting starts after each player is dealt his hole card. Hence there is one additional round of betting.

Unless this game is played in a liberal fashion it is no fun at all, since otherwise only those players fortunate enough to get an ace, king, queen or jack dealt to them stay in the pot at all. When played liberally it is fun, since you have the spectacle of players raising with a very low card on the theory that if the next card pairs them no one will suspect what they have. However, even in that type game there is still a great weakness—namely, that the

player who sits back and waits for an ace will
eventually wind up with all the money.

Mexican Five-Card Stud

In this game each card is dealt face down and
before each round of betting starts the players decide which card they will keep for their hole card.
There is a natural presumption that a player will
conceal as much of his strength as possible. In turn
this allows for some very interesting bluffs. For
example, a player starts with an ace and a deuce
and naturally turns up the deuce. He now gets a
three-spot, turns up the ace and proceeds to bet
exactly as if he had a pair of aces.

Joker Poker

In this game the joker is added to the regular
pack of fifty-two cards and a player may count it
as any card he desires—even one in his own hand.
Thus a player with four of a kind and the joker has
five of a kind—a new category which beats any
other. Or a player with the joker, the ace of hearts
and three other hearts has a double-ace flush, which
beats any other flush.

The purpose of playing with a joker, of course, is
to improve the hands. Hence, theoretically, since
the hands are better there will be more action, and
in Draw Poker it does work out that way to some
extent, although once a group becomes accustomed
to the addition of the joker they all increase their
minimum requirements for opening, staying, rais-

ing, etc., so that in reality there is little if any change effected in the game.

In Five-Card Stud, strangely enough, putting a joker in the pack greatly decreases the amount of action, since if the joker appears face up, anyone else who does not have a high pair immediately drops out; while if it doesn't appear, any player who takes any strong action is immediately suspected of having the joker in the hole.

The Bug

In this variation the joker may count only as an ace or to fill a straight or a flush. Thus a pair of aces and the Bug are three aces; a pair of kings and the Bug count merely as a pair with an ace kicker.

Strangely enough, the use of the Bug livens up Draw Poker more than the joker, the reason being that since it is not completely wild the fact that a player does not hold the Bug himself does not stop him from betting. Then, since there are now five aces in the deck, the number of times someone holds a pair of aces is greatly increased. Furthermore, the chance of getting a third ace in the draw to a pair of aces becomes about fifty per cent better than in straight poker.

Then the Bug fits in with all types of straight combinations. Thus, if you draw to a seven, eight, nine and the Bug, any jack, ten, eight or seven (one of sixteen cards) gives you your straight, while if you draw to a nine, eight, six and the Bug, you have twelve chances for success.

Then when we come to Stud Poker the Bug merely increases the value of all the other aces, since if you do have an ace your chance of pairing it is greatly increased. However, a word to the wise: In playing Stud Poker with the Bug do not get too enthusiastic about having a king in the hole. Remember there are five aces in the pack and only four kings.

CHAPTER VIII

Poker Probabilities and Mathematics

Introduction

To be a really good poker player it is essential to have a fair idea of the direct probabilities underlying various situations in poker in order to use them as a guide to one's general course of action. But one should always bear in mind that in the final bet or bets the psychology of one's opponents is much more important than any of the direct mathematical probabilities.

I was fortunate to learn this at the age of fifteen. In the fall of 1918 by dint of some judicious maneuvering I managed to get myself in the army. I wasn't much of a soldier but I did receive a thorough military training in the principles of poker, my chief instructor being an old sergeant who used to come out the big winner in practically every game. Naturally I made a study of the sergeant's military tactics and pretty soon I discovered his simple system.

The game was Table Stakes Stud, although the table stakes were commensurate with the soldiers' thirty dollars a month. Occasionally, however, after seven or eight of us had cornered most of the company's money, the game might run into fair figures.

My first line on the sergeant's theory came when a player showing the king, queen, jack and ten of spades tapped him and the sergeant called with a pair of threes and won a big pot. I asked him about that the next day and he said, "Well, in that spot this other fellow was going to bet whether he had them or not, and I couldn't afford not to call."

The next time we played I had aces back to back against his kings. Two other aces had appeared during the course of the early rounds, but when I tapped the sergeant on the last round he turned up the king he had in the hole and threw his hand away without hesitation. I didn't ask him why he did it because I didn't have to. I put two and two together and said to myself, "The sergeant didn't call because he figured it was such a foolish time to bluff that I must have that case ace in the hole."

The sergeant's theory—which might be summarized as, "To hell with the mathematics—it's the money that counts!"—has worked for me ever since. But, strangely enough, it proved his undoing in the final two-day game that preceded our discharge. By this time I had learned that he liked his theory so much that he made the mistake of *never departing from it in the slightest*. Accordingly, whenever he made a logical bet I called him, knowing he might be bluffing. But when he made an illogical one I dropped, knowing that he wasn't bluffing. Whenever it looked like a poor time for me to bluff him I did so with perfect safety; while if it looked like a good time for me to bluff him I'd have to have an "immortal" before I would throw a chip into the pot.

Mathematics of Draw Poker

There are 2,598,960 possible poker hands in a fifty-two-card deck. This is the number of combinations of fifty-two things taken five at a time and is equal to the product of the numbers fifty-two, fifty-one, fifty, forty-nine and forty-eight divided by the product of the numbers one, two, three, four and five. Table I shows the division of these hands into categories.

TABLE I

POSSIBLE POKER HANDS IN A FIFTY-TWO-CARD PACK

	Actual Number Possible	Expected Number in 10,000 Deals	Approximate Number of Times	
Straight flush	40	$\frac{1}{6}$	Once in 64,974	deals
Four of a kind	624	$2\frac{1}{2}$	" " 4,165	"
Full house	3,744	14	" " 694	"
Flush	5,108	20	" " 509	"
Straight	10,200	39	" " 256	"
Three of a kind	54,912	211	" " 48	"
Two pairs	123,552	475	" " 21	"
One pair	1,098,240	4,226	" " $2\frac{1}{2}$	"
No pair	1,302,540	5,012	" " 2	"
Total	2,598,960	10,000		

The above table is of no great value, although the second and third columns are valuable as a quick reference guide. However, the following table, which is derived directly from it, will prove quite valuable.

TABLE II

CHANCES OF HOLDING ANY PARTICULAR HAND OR BETTER IN FIRST FIVE CARDS

		Approximate Number of Times			Exact Chance
Any pair	or better	Once in	2	deals	.4988
Pair of jacks	" "	" "	5	"	.2062
Pair of queens	" "	" "	6	"	.1737
Pair of kings	" "	" "	7	"	.1412
Pair of aces	" "	" "	9	"	.1087
Two pairs	" "	" "	13	"	.0762
Three of a kind	" "	" "	35	"	.0287
Straight	" "	" "	132	"	.0076
Flush	" "	" "	270	"	.0037
Full house	" "	" "	588	"	.0017

The chance of holding any specified pair is .0325.

Let us now see what uses can be made of these tables:

We are playing a game of Jack Pots and the first player opens. We know from experience that this particular player considers a pair of queens or jacks too weak for an opening under the guns and he always sandbags with three of a kind or better. Hence he has opened on a pair of kings, a pair of aces or two pairs. From Table I the chance of holding exactly two pairs is .0475. From Table II the chance of holding a pair of aces is .0325, or holding aces or kings .0650. Hence the odds are roughly six hundred and fifty to four hundred and seventy-five, or slightly more than four to three, that he has opened on one pair only. If we do have any two pairs (even threes and deuces), the chances are that we have the better hand. Therefore, as a matter of strict mathematics, we should raise with any two pairs. Actually, however, a safety factor is desirable. Hence, if you will turn to the chapter on Draw Poker, you will find that I recommend nines up or better.

Now consider the player who opens in sixth or seventh position if he has any openers whatsoever. He may have jacks, kings, queens or aces, the chance of which is .1300; or he may have two pairs or better, the chance of which is .0762. In other words, it is almost two to one that he has opened with one pair, and now we can afford to raise with any two pairs and leave ourselves a reasonable margin of safety.

The following table is included for the benefit of those who like to play Draw Poker either with the low hand winning or the high and low hands dividing.

TABLE III

POSSIBLE HANDS OF LESS VALUE THAN ONE PAIR

Ace high	502,860
King high	335,580
Queen high	213,180
Jack high	127,500
Ten high	70,380
Nine high	34,680
Eight high	14,280
Seven high	4,080
Total	1,302,540

Two Pairs

There are seventy-eight possible combinations of
two pairs, ranging from the highest (aces and kings)
to the lowest (threes and deuces). Of these seventy-
eight combinations twelve are aces up, eleven kings
up, ten queens up, nine jacks up, etc.

Accordingly, it is important to note that if you
have tens and nines, which look like two fairly
good-sized pairs, actually the chances are that if
another player has two pairs, they will be better
than yours, the reason being that forty-two of the
seventy-eight combinations are jacks up or better.

The Draw

One of the oldest problems in the game is
whether or not to draw down to your hand. Thus a
player with a set of threes will frequently find it
profitable to draw but one card, while a player
with a pair may well desire to hold a kicker.

This holding of a kicker materially reduces your
chances of improving but at the same time adds a
decided deceptive value to your game. Thus here
are your chances:

TABLE IV

DRAWING THREE CARDS TO ONE PAIR

Odds Against Making	Any Improvement	Two Pairs	Three of a Kind	Full House	Four of a Kind
	$2\frac{1}{2}$ to 1	5 to 1	8 to 1	97 to 1	359 to 1

DRAWING TWO CARDS TO A PAIR AND AN ACE KICKER

Odds Against Making	Any Improvement	Aces Up	Another Pair	Three of a Kind	Full House	Four of a Kind
3 to 1	7½ to 1	17 to 1	12 to 1	118 to 1	1,080 to 1	

DRAWING TWO CARDS TO THREE OF A KIND

Odds Against Making	Any Improvement	Full House	Four of a Kind
	8½ to 1	15⅓ to 1	22½ to 1

DRAWING ONE CARD TO THREE OF A KIND AND A KICKER

Odds Against Making	Any Improvement	Full House	Four of a Kind
	11 to 1	14⅔ to 1	46 to 1

The preceding table shows that holding a kicker materially reduces your chances of improving your hand. Hence, if you do hold a kicker, it should be for some specific reason.

Incidentally, the odds against making a full house when you hold two pairs are approximately eleven to one.

Draws to Straights and Flushes

While I have already discussed the chances of making a straight or a flush on a one-card draw, I might as well summarize them here:

When you draw one card to an open-end straight flush it is twenty-two and a half to one against making a straight flush but only two to one against making a straight or better.

When you draw one card to an interior straight flush it is forty-six to one against making your straight flush and three to one against some pat hand.

In drawing to a four flush the odds are four and a half to one against success; in drawing to an open-end straight, five to one; and in drawing to an interior straight, eleven to one.

Freak Draws

I used to have a friend who claimed he could resist anything except cigarettes and temptation. I also know a lot of poker players who can avoid all bad plays except one—that is, they always draw two cards to a straight flush.

I admit this is quite a temptation. But before making this and similar draws you might bear in mind that the best combination is three in succession of the same suit open to two cards on either end, such as queen, jack, ten. Yet here the odds against your making a straight or better are eleven to one. With king, queen and jack of the same suit the odds against you go up to thirteen and a half to one. With ace, king and queen of the same suit the odds against you increase to twenty to one.

If you are foolish enough to try to draw two cards to just a flush, it is twenty-three to one against you. In drawing two cards to an open-end straight the odds against you are twenty-two to one.

Once in a while we see a desperation draw of four cards to an ace. Here it is three to one against making as good as a pair of aces and fourteen to one against making as good as aces up.

Probabilities of Five-Card Stud

As far as I know, no book on poker has ever given the probabilities in any game except Draw. However, I believe that the average Stud player would like to know something about what his chances are of pairing his hole card, etc., so I am giving a few figures.

First, let us consider the case when you have an ace in the hole and want to know just what your chance is of pairing that ace. Obviously all Stud probabilities are affected by exactly what cards have appeared around the table. Here are the probabilities:

TABLE V

	No Ace Showing	One Ace Showing
8-handed game	.200	.136
7-handed game	.195	.133
6-handed game	.191	.130
5-handed game	.187	.128

With two other aces showing, the chance of catching that case ace is approximately half that with one ace showing. Mathematically this is a very poor chance, but really good poker players stay for one card, anyway, because of the possible great element of surprise if they do catch that case ace.

After getting your third card your chance of pairing your ace on the last two cards is as follows:

TABLE VI

Number of Cards Shown by Other Players	No Aces Showing	One Ace Showing
12	.158	.107
10	.150	.101
8	.143	.096
6	.136	.092

Studying this table, we clearly see that if we happen to have a large hole card and no card of the same denomination has appeared, it is definitely worth while to stay and draw a fourth card, provided: (1) the betting has not become too heavy; (2) no one shows an open pair or a card higher in denomination than our hole card.

Another important problem in Five-Card Stud, where knowledge of the probabilities involved is a great help, occurs when your first three cards include a small pair and you suspect that the player betting against you already has a larger pair.

In this situation, as in all such situations, the more cards you have seen that do not pair your own, the better your chance of improving; while if you can account for even one card that might help you, your chance is greatly decreased.

The following table will act as a rough guide.

TABLE VII

CHANCES OF IMPROVING WHEN YOUR FIRST THREE CARDS ARE A PAIR AND AN ODD CARD

Number of Cards You Have Seen Other Than Your Own	Chance of Improving if None of These Cards Is the Same Denomination as Your Pair or Your Odd Card	Chance of Improving if One of These Cards Is the Same Denomination as Your Pair or Odd Card
10	.292	.250
8	.283	.243
6	.274	.236

Summarizing the above, we have as a simple rule of thumb that the odds are about two and a half to one against our improving if we have seen no card of the same denomination as our own but slightly over three to one against our improving if we have seen one such card.

Down-the-River or Seven-Card Stud

In this game the average player would like to know what his chances are of making his straights and flushes starting with various combinations. Accordingly, we present Tables VIII and IX.

In studying Table VIII the first thing we note is that if we start with three cards of the same suit it is about four and a half to one against our making the flush. Now if our next card is also the same suit, our chance is almost even money; while if it doesn't help us, the chances against us increase to nine to one. Accordingly, if my three cards are all

TABLE VIII

CHANCES OF MAKING A FLUSH

You Hold	Chance of Eventually Making a Flush
Three cards of one suit	.180
" " " " " and one odd card	.106
" " " " " " two odd cards	.042
Four " " " "	.472
" " " " " and one odd card	.350
" " " " " " two odd cards	.196

TABLE IX

CHANCES OF MAKING A STRAIGHT

You Hold	Chance of Eventually Making a Straight
Q, J, 10	.190
Q, J, 10, x	.112
Q, J, 10, x, x	.044
Q, J, 10, 9	.429
Q, J, 10, 9, x or A, Q, J, 10, 8	.315
Q, J, 10, 9, x, x or A, Q, J, 10, 8, x	.174
Q, J, 10, 8	.270
Q, J, 10, 8, x	.179
Q, J, 10, 8, x, x	.087
K, Q, J or 4, 3, 2	.131
K, Q, J, x or 4, 3, 2, x	.076
A, K, Q or 3, 2, A	.072
A, K, Q, x or 3, 2, A, x	.040

in the same suit, unless the pot is raised I am going to stay and draw a fourth card. But if that fourth card is not in my suit, my participation in that particular pot is ended unless that fourth card happens to give me a pair, in which case I may trail along, depending on just how much strength is shown by the other players.

The queen, jack, ten is given as an example of any three cards in succession which may become a straight upon the addition of two cards at either end or one card at each end. Players will do well to note how much less the chance is when starting with king, queen, jack or four, three, two.

It is further worthy of note that, as in the case with three to a flush, if your fourth card does not help you there is little point in staying further, since the chances against your eventually making a straight have increased from four to one to eight to one.

TABLE X

CHANCE OF MAKING A FULL HOUSE OR BETTER

You Hold	Chance of Eventually Making a Full House or Better
Three of a kind	.402
Three of a kind and one odd card	.389
Three of a kind " two odd cards	.333
Three of a kind " three odd cards	.217
Pair and an odd card	.073
" " two odd cards	.051
" " three odd cards	.026
Two pairs	.196
" " and odd card	.124
" " " two odd cards	.087

Chance of making four of a kind starting with three of a kind is .082.

The above figures are very instructive. Thus three of a kind is a very good high hand. First, there is a fine chance that even without improvement you will win the pot. Second, even though you have but one card left to get, the odds are less than four to one against your making either a full house or four of a kind.

However, in High-Low any three of a kind becomes much less valuable because you have practically no chance whatsoever of winning low, and hence the best you can hope for is to take half the pot.

On the other hand, it will be noted that two pairs are by no means anything to get too optimistic about. In the first place, even if your first four cards are two pairs, the odds are still more than four to one against your eventually making a full house; while with two pairs and an odd card the chances are seven to one against you. Although two pairs may win the pot, remember no guarantee goes with them.

Finally, in studying possibilities for High-Low, it should be noted that holding a pair and an odd card, your chance of eventually coming out with a full house is less than one in thirteen. Therefore, unless you have possibilities for low, the fact that you have a pair does not justify your staying for a fourth card in a High-Low game.

The following table is worth a considerable amount of study. In going over it it will, of course, be noted that many combinations of cards give the same chances of making a seven, eight or nine low

Table XI

HIGH–LOW SEVEN–CARD STUD

You Hold	Chance of Making a Seven Low	Chance of Making an Eight Low or Better	Chance of Making a Nine Low or Better
7, 3, 2	.190	.333	.490
7, 3, 2, x	.112	.209	.330
7, 3, 2, x, x	.044	.089	.148
7, 3, 2, 4	.429	.587	.724
7, 3, 2, 4, x	.315	.450	.585
7, 3, 2, 4, x, x	.174	.261	.348
4, 3, 2	.131	.285	.469
4, 3, 2, x	.076	.177	.299
5, 4, 3	.072	.233	.411
5, 4, 3, x	.040	.144	.275

as do seven, three, two, etc. For instance, when you start with a seven, three, two, in order to make a seven low you must get two out of three specified cards, in this instance the four, five and six. If you start with seven, six, two you must also get two out of three specified cards, in this case a three, four and five. However, it is obvious that seven, three, two is a slightly more valuable holding for low than seven, six, two.

Starting with four, three, two, your chances of making a low hand are less than when you start with seven, three, two since you are more likely to wind up with a straight. Similarly, with a three, four, five or four, five, six your chances are further reduced. As against that, the chance that you will make a straight and win high is increased.

Incidentally, many readers will wonder just what the chance is of making both a seven low and a straight, starting with a holding such as two, three, four. The answer is .024 or one in forty. However, the chance of making an eight low and a straight is almost twice as good, and an eight low and a straight is very likely to win both ways.

Now for a little word of advice. Holding seven, three, two, x, your chance of winding up with an eight low or better is .209. Holding seven, three, two, four, the chance is .587. Accordingly, if you start with three good cards and draw something like a king, whereas one of your opponents shows two low cards, you can see what a great advantage he has against you if he has two perfect cards in the hole. However, in spite of that, if he does not bet too strongly you may stay for another card, because if you get a good one and he gets a bad one, you have caught him.

However, let us look down the table a little further. Holding seven, three, two, x, x, your chance of getting eight low or better is .089. Holding seven, three, two, four, x, it is .450. Accordingly, if you find that two of your first five cards are bad, there is little point in continuing in the pot if any other player shows but one bad card because the odds against you are entirely too great.

CHAPTER IX

Problems

THE FOLLOWING PROBLEMS are all taken from actual poker games I have played in or seen. The readers may study them, make up their own solutions and check with the answers.

Problem 1

The game is seven-handed Table Stakes Stud with the dealer anteing one chip. It is the last hand of the evening. In addition to the regular ante each player antes two chips, so there are fifteen chips in the pot. Mr A, a fair poker player of a rather straightforward nature, is a small loser, has an ace showing and bets two chips. Three others call, including B, who shows a five, and there are now twenty-three chips in the pot. The next card A draws a four, B an eight. A bets forty chips; B calls and the others drop. There are now one hundred and three chips in the pot. Each player receives a ten. A bets one hundred chips. B calls. There are now two hundred and eighty-three chips in the pot and A and B each have about five hundred chips left in front of them. On the fifth card A draws another four-spot and B a queen. A now bets one hundred and twenty chips. B has a pair of fives and calls.

QUESTION 1. Was B right?

QUESTION 2. Assuming B was wrong, what was A's hole card?

ANSWER, QUESTION 1: B should not have called.

ANSWER, QUESTION 2: A's hole card was a four-spot.

Let's consider the whole sequence of betting. On the first round, with fifteen chips in the pot, A bet only two chips. With a very tricky person that might mean aces back to back, but with a man of A's nature it could only mean that he had a low card in the hole. On the second card A bet about twice the size of the pot. Now he is either bluffing absolutely or has made fours. On the third round A bets approximately the size of the pot. It is now almost sure that he has fours, and finally, on the last round, A bets considerably less than the size of the pot. This last bet is the final confirmation of the fact that A now has a sure thing. Had he tapped, conceivably he might be bluffing, but this small bet is an obvious effort to coax a few more chips out of B.

Problem 2

The game is Table Stakes High-Low Five-Card Stud and everybody has over a thousand chips in front of him.

Player A shows a queen and opens for a chip.

Player B raises ten chips with an eight. Players C, D and E, showing a six, five and three, each call. Player A, with a four-spot in the hole, raises back fifty chips in an effort to convey the impression that he holds queens back to back.

On the next round everyone draws a low card. Player A bets two hundred chips. Players B and C call; D and E drop. On the fourth card B draws an ace, C a king and A another low card. Players B and C both check. What should Player A do?

ANSWER: Player A should check also.

This problem is taken from an actual game and A made this brilliant play. His reasoning was that by checking he indicated clearly to his opponents that he had a queen in the hole and was afraid to bet for fear that one of the opponents had made a higher pair.

Each of the players now received a low card. The man with the ace showing checked. The player with the king, who had a low card in the hole, now bet, figuring that A surely had a pair of queens. A just called, still concealing the fact that he held an "immortal" for low. And B, who happened to have an ace in the hole in addition to the ace showing, now raised. C, with the king, raised back. A merely called, and now the player with the ace tapped. C called and A called, thereby winning one half of a very large pot.

Of course if A had bet right out on the fourth card he might have coaxed C to come in for all his chips anyway, but I doubt it.

Problem 3

In a seven-handed game of Limit Draw Poker you are first man and open the pot with fours and deuces. The sixth player and the dealer both call. You draw one card and check. The sixth man draws one card and bets the limit. The dealer draws three cards and raises.

You look at your hand and find that you have drawn a third four, thereby giving you a full house. What should you do?

ANSWER: Your correct play is to call. The man who stayed before the draw and drew one card obviously had either two pairs or a four flush, because if he had held three of a kind he would have raised before the draw. Now the only reason for his bet must be: (a) he has made a pat hand; (b) he is bluffing.

The dealer, who drew three cards, obviously started with a high pair and now could only be raising the one-card draw (a) as a bluff; (b) because he himself had made a full house or four of a kind. If he has made a full house he will undoubtedly beat you, but the chance that he is bluffing is sufficient to warrant your putting in the chips to call. But a raise would be nothing but pure philanthropy.

Problem 4

You are playing Jack Pots. You are the dealer and hold a pair of threes, a pair of deuces and an ace. The first player opens for the size of the pot. Everyone drops but the player immediately to your right, who raises the limit. What should you do?

ANSWER: You should drop. The man who raises is either bluffing or has you beaten. But even if he is bluffing, there is still a very good chance that the opener will be able to beat your two very small pairs.

Incidentally, with this hand the fact that your odd card is an ace is a warning signal, since it decreases the chance that one of the other players is doing his betting on a pair of aces and hence increases the chance that his holding is two pairs or better.

Problem 5

You are playing Deuces Wild and hold two deuces, a seven, a six and a five. The hand is opened. You raise. The opener stays for the raise and draws two cards. What do you do?

ANSWER: You stand pat. The chances are that he has a high three of a kind, and the odds are against his improving.

Problem 6

You are playing Deuces Wild. Once more you have two deuces, a seven, a six and a five. The pot is opened. You raise. The dealer raises you and the opener stays for the raise. You call. The opener now draws two cards. What do you do?

ANSWER: Draw three cards to your pair of deuces. Obviously the player who raised you holds a better hand than a straight.

Problem 7

You are playing Jack Pots. The pot is opened by the first man. You stay with a pair of aces, a king, a six and a three. Everyone else drops. The opener draws three cards. What do you do?

ANSWER: You should hold two aces and the king as a kicker. While holding the king kicker slightly reduces your chances of improving, there is a distinct possibility that your opponent holds the other two aces. In this case your king kicker is very likely to win the pot for you.

Problem 8

The game is Table Stakes Seven-Card Stud with high and low dividing the pot. With a thousand chips in front of you you have two kings in the hole and a king showing. The dealer has anted five chips. You bet five chips and four players stay, leaving a total of thirty chips in the pot. You receive a nine and check. The player to your left, who now shows the seven and six of spades, bets thirty chips. Everyone else drops. What should you do?

ANSWER: Your correct play is to drop also. True, the odds are greatly in favor of your winning high. But if you do win high, all you gain is fifteen chips, representing one half of the thirty in the pot prior to the thirty-chip bet. But if you stay for the thirty-chip bet you will find yourself more or less committed to stay for a one-hundred-chip bet on the next card and eventually will have to risk your entire thousand chips. Then if the other player wins both ways (and that is a distinct possibility), you will have lost a thousand in an effort to gain fifteen.

Problem 9

You are playing High-Low Seven-Card Stud, Table Stakes. It is the last card and there are about six hundred chips in the pot. Player A to your left (a conservative player) shows two nines, an eight and a seven and bets five hundred chips. Player B at your right shows the ace, jack, eight of hearts and six of diamonds and calls. You show a seven, a six, a four and a deuce and have two other sevens and a deuce in the hole.

You have two thousand chips in front of you; Player A has more; Player B has only about fifty chips left. What do you do?

ANSWER: Your correct play is to pass. The reason is as follows: Player A's bet could indicate but one thing—a full house—because since he is a conservative player he would never make a bet on a straight with another player showing the ace, jack and eight of hearts.

Player B's call may be based on a flush and the hope that A is bluffing, or on an eight low and the hope that you have nothing in the hole to help the low cards you show. Or it might (and this last possibility is very remote) be based on a very big full house.

In any event your seven full is no good for high, and the best you can make for low is a pair of deuces. Therefore, if B is calling on a flush he will still beat you for low. Accordingly, your only real chance of winning any part of the pot is that both A and B have full houses. This is so unlikely that you should not call.

Problem 10

You are playing Table Stakes Five-Card Stud with an ante of five chips by the dealer. You have fifty chips in front of you. On the first round the player to your right is high with a ten-spot and opens for five chips. You stay with an eight up and a king in the hole, as do two other players, so that there are twenty-five chips in the pot. On the next card you catch an eight. Everybody else catches a low card. You bet twenty chips. Everyone drops but the player with ten, who now raises you the remaining twenty-five. What should you do?

ANSWER: You should call. In so doing you are risking twenty-five chips to gain ninety—the amount in the pot at this time. Hence you are getting almost four to one for your money, and the odds against your making two pairs or three of a kind are only about two and a half to one. Of course your opponent may also improve, but to offset that unfavorable possibility there is the favorable one that he may be bluffing.

CHAPTER X

Poker: Definitions, Glossary and Laws

Laws of Poker

Unlike bridge, where the laws as established by the Whist Club of New York have been accepted as standard for many years, there is no official law-making body in poker. Each locality and each game has its own local rules, which in general follow those published in the various "Hoyles" or books of games. The laws as presented here are the result of years of study and consultation with poker players all over the country. They are intended to cover the game as generally played today and may safely be adopted as standard.

Description of Game, Preliminary Definitions and Glossary

Poker is a game of betting, played with chips which may or may not represent money. In Draw Poker there are two rounds of betting; in Five-Card Stud there are four rounds; in other variations there may be as many as eight or nine rounds.

The following definitions apply to all variations:

1. POT: All the chips that are bet on any particular hand go into the pot and at the conclusion of the hand become the property of the winner or winners.

2. ANTE: Chips placed in the pot before the deal.

3. BET: Any number of chips placed by a player in the pot is known as a bet.

4. RAISE: Any bet in excess of the last previous bet. Also the amount of the excess.

5. CALL: Any bet exactly equal to the last previous bet.

6. ANNOUNCED BET: Announcement by a player to the effect that he is betting so much, raising so much or calling is just as valid as if he puts the chips in the pot. *Exception:* In a Table Stakes game, if a player announces a bet or raise in excess of the number of chips he has in front of him he is merely betting all his chips.

7. PASS: When it is a player's turn to bet, if he is not willing to call or raise the last preceding bet he must pass. A player who once passes has no further interest in the pot and should immediately throw his hand away.

8. CHECK: The first bettor may check, in which case each succeeding player has the same privilege until a bet is made. A player who has checked retains the right to raise or call any bet made. If all players check, the round of betting is completed.

9. ROUND OF BETTING: A round of betting

continues until each player has either passed or
called the last bet or raise.

10. SHOWDOWN: After the last round of betting each player remaining in the pot places his
hand face up on the table and the best hand wins
the pot. The cards speak for themselves, and even
though a player overlooks his own winning hand,
it is the duty of the other players to give him the
pot. In case the last bet has not been called, there
is no showdown. When there is a showdown the
hands of all players remaining in the pot must be
shown in full to any player who demands to see
them, even though the player who makes the de-
mand is not in the pot.

11. LIMIT: The maximum amount which any
player may raise the previous bet.

12. TABLE STAKES (more properly, Table
Stakes Limit): This means that the limit of chips
which a player may bet in any pot is represented
by the number of chips he had on the table at the
start of the hand.

13. POT LIMIT: In this game the limit at any
time is the number of chips in the pot, including
those necessary to call the last previous bet. *Example:* There are five chips in the pot. Player A
bets five chips, making ten in the pot. Now Player
B wishes to raise. He first puts in five chips to
call A's bet. This makes fifteen in the pot, and he
may now raise fifteen.

14. TAP: In Table Stakes when a player says,
"I tap," he means he is betting all his chips. When
he says, "I tap you," referring to another player,

he means he is betting a number of chips equal to the ones in front of the other player.

15. SIDE POT or SIDE MONEY: This occurs in Table Stakes and may best be defined by means of an example: A, B, C and D are in the pot. A has four hundred chips, B three hundred and fifty, C two hundred and fifty and D one hundred. A now says, "I tap," which means he is betting all his chips. B, C and D call for what they have. D has the fewest chips—one hundred. Therefore D's chips and one hundred each from A, B and C go into the main pot. C has two hundred and fifty chips. C's remaining one hundred and fifty go into a side pot and are matched by one hundred and fifty of B's and one hundred and fifty of A's. This makes four hundred and fifty chips for the first side pot. B has one hundred chips more. These are matched by one hundred of A's and form the second side pot, and A now takes back the fifty chips that he has left over.

16. DIVISION OF SIDE POT OR SIDE MONEY: The side pot or pots may only be taken by players who have an interest therein. Let us go back to our previous example. If either A or B has the best hand he takes all the pot and all the side money. If D has the best hand and C the second best and A the third, D wins the main pot, C the first side pot and A the second side pot. If C has the best hand he wins the main pot and the first side pot. *This method of division of side money does not apply in High-Low Poker.*

17. PREMIUMS or ROYALTIES: In some

games it is customary to reward extraordinary hands by paying a premium. In this event each player pays the premium whether or not he was in the pot.

18. FOUL HAND: A hand which has forfeited all interest in the pot.

Additional Poker Terms

1. BACKING IN: Coming into the pot after checking.

2. BACK TO BACK: In Five-Card Stud when a player's hole card pairs his first up card he is said to have a pair "back to back."

3. BOBTAIL: Four cards to a straight open on each end. *Example*: Six, seven, eight, nine.

4. BUCK: The buck is a token usually used to liven up the game of Draw Poker. Initially it goes to the winner of the first pot. When it becomes the turn of the player with the buck to deal he may either pass the buck to the player at his left or put the buck in the center and name what variation of poker he will deal. Of course the buck then goes to the winner of that pot, who has the same right when it becomes his deal.

5. DEAD HAND: In a Table Stakes game once a player has wagered all his chips he becomes what is known as a "dead hand" since he can do no more betting.

6. FOUR FLUSH: Four cards of the same suit.

7. FREE RIDE: The dead hand receives a "free ride" since, irrespective of what the other players

bet, he is entitled to stay in the pot until the finish.

8. HOLE CARD or HOLE CARDS: The concealed card or cards in Stud.

9. IMMORTAL: Any hand in a Stud game which is certain to win, irrespective of what card or cards the other players have in the hole.

10. IN THE HOLE: The hole card is "in the hole."

11. KITTY, FEEDING THE KITTY, etc.: In many games it is customary to keep a kitty, which receives one or more chips from the pot under certain conditions. The kitty then pays the expenses of the game, and the balance is either given to the big loser or divided among the losers.

12. OPEN PAIR: An exposed pair in Stud.

13. PAT HAND: A straight or better.

14. ROODLES: A roodle hand is one in which the stakes are temporarily increased. Thus, in many games of Draw Poker it is customary to increase the limit for one round following the holding of any four of a kind or better.

15. SANDBAGGING: When a player merely checks or calls with a good hand in the hope that he will be able to raise later he is "sandbagging."

16. SHORT PAIR: In Jack Pots any pair lower than jacks.

17. STANDING PAT: Not drawing any cards.

18. STAY: To call.

19. UNDER THE GUNS: The first player or players to act are said to be "under the guns."

20. UP CARD or UP CARDS: The exposed card or cards in Stud.

Laws

The Poker Hand

A poker hand consists of five cards. In variations where a player is dealt more than five cards he uses the best five to make his poker hand.

Rank of Cards

Regular poker is played with a standard fifty-two-card deck; the cards rank as in bridge, i.e., the ace high, the king next, etc. There is an exception, however, in that the ace is counted as a one with a combination of two, three, four, five to form a straight.

All suits rank the same.

Rank of Hands

Poker hands are ranked in nine categories, any hand in one category outranking all hands in a lower category. These categories are as follows:

1. Straight flush: Five cards in sequence of the same suit. (The Royal Flush is simply the highest possible straight flush—i.e., A, K, Q, J, 10 in one suit.)

2. Four of a kind and one odd card.

3. Full house: Three of one kind and two of another.

4. Flush: Five cards of the same suit.

5. Straight: Five cards in sequence.

6. Three of a kind and two odd cards.

7. Two pairs and an odd card.

8. One pair and three odd cards.

9. No pair.

Between two hands in the same category the relative rank is determined as follows:

Categories 1 and 5: The top card. For example, the highest straight is A, K, Q, J, 10; the lowest, 5, 4, 3, 2, A.

Category 2: The higher four of a kind.

Categories 3 and 6: The higher three of a kind.

Category 7: The highest pair. Thus aces and deuces outrank kings and queens. If each player has the same high pair, the second pair determines. If each player has the same two pairs, the odd card.

Category 8: The higher pair. If each player has the same pair, the highest outside card. If those tie, the next highest, etc.

Categories 4 and 9: The highest card. If they are identical, the next highest, etc.

Local Option Hands

There are any number of additional combinations of cards which are given rank in various localities. Some of these are the Dog, the Tiger, the Skeet, the Kilter, the Cat-hop, the Mississippi Bearcat, the Blaze, etc. The only ones which are used to any extent at all are the Dog and the Tiger. They are:

1. Big Tiger: A king to an eight with no pair. Ranks below a flush.

2. Little Tiger: An eight to a three with no pair. Ranks below a Big Tiger.

3. Big Dog: Ace to a nine with no pair. Ranks below a Little Tiger.

4. Little Dog: Seven to a two with no pair. Ranks below a Big Dog and above a straight.

The Joker

The game may be played with a joker. In this event the joker may be counted as any card, even one held by the player who holds the joker. Thus four of a kind and the joker count as five of a kind. This makes the highest hand and outranks any straight flush. The joker may also be used with a combination of cards, such as the ace, eight, seven and six of hearts to form a double-ace flush. This double-ace flush will outrank any other flush.

The Bug

The Bug is a joker without full privileges. It counts as an additional ace and may also be used to make up any straight or flush. Thus the Bug and a 6, 7, 8, 9 constitute a straight. But the Bug, three sixes and a ten merely count as three sixes since the Bug is not strictly a wild card.

The Stripped Deck

The lower cards may be taken out of the deck if desired. In this instance the ace still counts as a one at the bottom of a straight. Thus, if the deuces and treys are out of the deck, a 7, 6, 5, 4, A is a straight.

Wild Cards

Any card or cards may be counted as wild, in which case they have the same rights as jokers. If all of one rank—say the deuces—are wild, it is the same as playing with the stripped deck and four additional jokers.

Preliminaries to the Game

Number of Players

Any number of players from two up may play, although it is inadvisable to have more than eight, and seven constitutes the best game.

The Banker

The banker takes charge of and distributes the chips. However, unless otherwise provided, in the event of a bookkeeping error all players share an equal responsibility for the bank.

Choice of Seats

In general the players simply sit where they choose, the banker usually being given first choice.

First Deal

Any player picks up the deck and proceeds to deal the cards around, the first player who is dealt a jack becoming dealer. After that the deal passes in rotation to the left.

Conditions of the Game

Before start of play the following points should be definitely determined:

1. The value of the chips.
2. The ante.
3. The limit.
4. In the event of Table Stakes the conditions under which a player may (a) place more chips on the table; (b) withdraw chips from the table.[1]

Shuffle and Cut

Any player may shuffle the cards, the dealer having last right. The cards must then be offered to the player at the dealer's right for a cut. He is not obliged to cut, but if he declines to do so, any other player may claim the right.

Misdeal

In case of a misdeal the same player deals again with the same pack. A misdeal occurs:

1. If any card is exposed in cutting or reuniting the packs.
2. If any card is found faced in the pack prior to the start of the betting.
3. If two or more cards are exposed during the deal.
4. If at any time prior to the next hand it is proven that the pack was imperfect.

[1] In most Table Stakes games chips once in play may never be withdrawn.

5. If the wrong player deals and attention is called to that fact by a player who has not looked at any of his cards.

Card Exposed During Deal

In Stud Poker if a player's hole card is exposed during the deal, he takes it face up and simply receives his next card face down.

In Draw Poker if one of the player's cards is exposed during the deal, he must take it.

Bet Out of Turn

A bet out of turn is temporarily canceled and the betting reverts to the proper player. Then when it comes the turn to bet of the player who has bet out of turn he must:

1. If no bet has been made in the meanwhile, make the same bet he made out of turn.

2. If a bet smaller than the bet made out of turn has been made, he must raise to the extent of the out-of-turn bet.

3. If the preceding bet was raised to an amount exactly equal to his bet out of turn, he must call.

4. If the preceding bet was raised in excess of the amount bet out of turn, he must either (a) put in an amount equal to his bet out of turn and withdraw from the pot, or (b) call or (c) raise.

Raise Out of Turn

The same rules apply as for a bet out of turn.

Call Out of Turn

A call out of turn is temporarily canceled and the betting reverts to the proper player. Then, when it becomes the turn of the player who has called out of turn to bet he must call if there has been no raise. If there has been a raise, he must (a) put in the amount of his out-of-turn call and withdraw from the pot or (b) call.

Pass Out of Turn

If a player passes out of turn, his hand immediately becomes foul and he has no further interest in the pot.

Irregularities in the Betting

If a player announces that he is betting or raising a certain number of chips and at the same time places a different number of chips in the pot, he is betting or raising the amount he announces and must correct the number placed in the pot. *Exception:* In a Table Stakes game if a player puts his whole stack in the pot, he is deemed to be betting that amount even though he makes some other announcement.

Irregularities in the Hand[2]

Any hand of more than five cards, any part of which has been looked at, is foul, and the player

[2]In many variations of poker a proper hand consists of more or less than five cards. In such games, of course, substitute the proper number

holding it forfeits all right in that particular pot.

If a player with less than five cards looks at any part of his hand he must play through the rest of the pot with the insufficient number of cards. Thus he cannot make a straight, a flush or a full house. (Note: Under the old laws of poker a hand of less than five cards is foul also. In my opinion and in that of all my consultants forcing a player to play with four cards is sufficient penalty.)

If a player who has not looked at his hand has less than five cards, the dealer must complete his hand with a card or cards from the top of the pack.

If a player who has not looked at his hand has more than five cards, the dealer must draw a card from his hand and place it on the bottom of the pack.

If one player who has not looked at his hand has six cards and another four, the player with four must draw a card from the player with six.

If two players have four cards or two players six, it is a misdeal.

A deal out of turn or with the wrong pack must be stopped, except that no player who has looked at a card may call attention to this irregularity.

The Draw

If during the course of the draw a card is discovered faced in the pack, it is simply shown to all

of cards for five. Similarly, in the various Stud games the player should have a certain number of cards in the hole. If he happens to have more or less than the proper number, the same rules apply.

the players and placed among the discards, and the players receive their next cards in regular rotation.

If any card is faced by the dealer during the draw, it is also placed in the discards. In this event, however, the player who would have received it draws the card to replace it *after all other players have drawn.*

The last card may not be dealt. If, as is sometimes the case, there are no cards left to allow the last players to draw, the other players' discards and the passed hands are shuffled and dealt.

If a player asks for too few cards and has not looked at any of them, he may correct the error before the next player has drawn. Otherwise he must play through with the insufficient number of cards.

If a player asks for too many cards and looks at any of them, his hand is foul. Otherwise he may correct the error before the next player has drawn. If the next player has drawn, he may correct himself by discarding additional cards from his original hand.

If a player asks for the right number of cards but receives the wrong number and looks at any of them, the same rules shall apply as if he had asked for the wrong number. Otherwise the error must be corrected the moment the dealer's attention is called to it, whether or not the next player has drawn.

If the dealer draws too few cards he must play with the insufficient number. If he draws too many and looks at any of them, his hand is foul. Otherwise he may correct himself by discarding additional cards from his original hand.

If a player allows the man on his left to draw out of turn he must either play his hand without drawing or abandon it. If he has discarded he must play with the cards he has left.

Once a player has drawn, no information may be given as to how many cards he has drawn, except that any player still in the pot who has not made a bet may ask the dealer how many he (the dealer) has drawn.

Betting before the Draw

The rules for betting before the draw depend on which of several varieties of Draw Poker is being played. The following are the four principal variations and the rules covering them:

1. *Straight Draw:* Commencing at the dealer's left, each player either checks or opens. Once the pot is opened, succeeding players must either call, raise or pass.

2. *Jack Pots:* In this game the opener must have a pair of jacks or better. However, a player has the right of checking openers if he desires.

In either Straight Draw or Jack Pot, if all players check, the deal passes to the next player and there is an additional ante.

3. *Pass Out:* In this game there is no privilege of checking before the draw. A player must either bet or pass. If everyone but the dealer passes, he takes the pot.

4. *Blind Opening:* In this game the player to the

dealer's left is compelled to open the pot f
specified amount, irrespective of his hand. In s
games the second player is now compelled to
blind.

Betting after the Draw

Irrespective of which variation of Draw
is being played, after the draw the man who
the first bet is known as the "opener," and it
turn to bet first. He may check if he desires.

Showing Openers

In a Jack Pot, if the opener wins without
called, he must show enough of his hand to in
that he held proper openers, but need not sh
whole hand. If he cannot show openers, all
is left in the pot, the deal passes, there is
ditional ante and the next winner takes every
If during the course of the betting the
decides to drop out, he must show that
openers. If he is unable to show openers, any
remaining in the pot is privileged to an
"I have openers." In this case the play
makes this announcement takes the place
original opener and the betting continues
ever, if no player is able or willing to state
has openers, all players except the man who
irregularly withdraw whatever they have
the pot. The irregular opener, however, m
his bet or bets in the pot and the deal pas
In the event of a showdown, in which

the opener nor any of the other players can show openers, the best hand other than that of the irregular opener wins the pot.

Splitting Openers

The opener has the right to discard part of his openers without any announcement if he desires, but in this event must be able to show from his discards that he had openers. Accordingly, it is customary (whether or not he has split openers) for him to place his discards under the chips in the pool where they may be available for inspection. In the event of a final call, if the opener at that time has the best hand but is unable to show that he had openers, he loses the pot. (This contingency only arises when the opener has split his openers in order to draw to a flush or straight and has made his hand but has failed to protect his discards.)

Stud Poker

In Stud Poker each player is dealt one card face down and one card face up. There is a round of betting. Those remaining in the pot receive another card face up. There is another round of betting, and so on until each player has a total of five cards, thereby making a total of four rounds of betting. In each round of betting the first bet goes to the man who has the highest holding in sight on the table. If two or more players show the same, the one of them nearest the dealer's left is first bettor.

Check

On the first round of betting the players in turn must either bet or pass. After the first round they have the privilege of checking.

Cards Exposed

If a card is exposed in any manner before a round of betting is completed, the round is nevertheless completed. Then the dealer buries one card for each player remaining in the pot, the exposed card or cards being included among the buried cards, and continues the deal.

Down-the-River (Seven-Card Stud)

In this variation of Stud there are five rounds of betting, each player eventually having seven cards. The five of these seven which constitute the best poker hand are his hand. As a start, two cards are dealt face down and one face up to each player. Then three more are dealt face up and the last card is given face down. In this game, if the last card is exposed, the same rule shall apply as to cards exposed during the draw in Draw Poker—the card so exposed must be buried and the player receives another last card after all other players have received theirs.

Other Variations

It is possible to play six-card, eight-card or even ten-card Stud if you wish. Any particular number of cards may be dealt face up or face down as desired.

Mexican Stud

In Mexican Stud each player is dealt the first two cards face down. Before the betting the players in turn expose one card. After the first round of betting the next card is dealt face down, and the players again have the privilege of deciding which card they wish to expose. Otherwise the game is the same as straight Stud.

Spit-in-the-Ocean

In Spit-in-the-Ocean a card is dealt face up in the center and each player uses this card as the fifth card in his hand, four being dealt directly to him. In most instances it is customary to play the center card and all like it wild.

Cincinnati

In this game each player is dealt five cards and there are five cards in the center which are turned up one at a time, a round of betting following the turning up of each card. These five belong to all players, who combine any of them they wish with any cards from their own hand to form the best poker hand.

Variations

In Spit-in-the-Ocean and Cincinnati there are any number of variations possible since the players may be given any number of cards in their hands and any number may be dealt on the table. Then the game may be played with wild cards. For instance, the lowest card in the center and all like it might be played as wild.

Low Poker

Low Poker is played under exactly the same rules as High Poker except that the lowest poker hand wins—not the highest. Thus a seven, five, four, three, two is a perfect low.

Low Poker with the Ace Low

In this variation of Low Poker the ace ranks as a one and the perfect low is a six, four, three, two, one.

Supplementary Laws

There are so many variations of poker that it is impossible to cover every situation by strict laws. The following are a few situations that have caused arguments from time to time, and I am discussing them here with my own recommendations, which need not be followed if the local custom is different.

1. *Impossible Call:* In a Stud game, when the last player to act is beaten in sight but calls by mistake he should be given his money back, since there was no conceivable manner in which he could gain by his call.

2. *Folding a Beaten Hand:* After the last card is dealt in Five-Card Stud, even though a player's hand is beaten in sight, he should make no move

to fold it except in his proper turn, following a bet by another player.

3. *Running Out of Cards:* In an eight-handed game of Seven-Card Stud it may be found that there are not enough cards for each player in the pot to receive his final card. In this case, instead of dealing a final hole card to each player, one card is dealt face up in the center and belongs to all players.

4. *Flashing a Card:* It frequently happens that the dealer flashes one or more of the cards of a player's draw in Draw Poker or the final concealed card in a game such as Down-the-River. In this instance, if no one in the pot except the player receiving the card can see it, the player must take it. If anyone else sees it, however, he must speak up, whereupon the card becomes exposed.

Laws of High-Low Poker

1. The laws of regular poker shall apply to High-Low Poker, except that in High-Low Poker the highest poker hand and the lowest poker hand divide the pot.

2. *Odd Chips:* If after the division there is an odd chip left over, it either goes to the high hand or is put in the kitty.

3. *Ties:* In the event that two hands tie for either high or low the tying players each receive one fourth.

4. *Limit:* If High-Low is played with a fixed limit it is necessary to restrict the maximum num-

ber of raises. This may be done according to one of two methods: (a) Place a limit on the number of chips a player may bet on any one round; (b) Place a limit on the number of raises on any one round.

5. Unless otherwise provided, in High-Low *Five-Card* Stud any player, before receiving his last card, has the right to turn up his hole card and ask for the last card down.

6. In Seven-Card Stud and similar games in which a player has more than five cards, a player has two distinct hands: (1) A high hand, represented by the five cards which form the highest possible poker hand; (2) A low hand, represented by the five cards which form the lowest possible poker hand. In seven-card High-Low at least three cards, of necessity, must be included in both the player's high hand and low hand.

A player may win both high and low and thereby take the whole pot.

7. *Side Money:* In a Table Stakes game the side money is divided as follows:

(a) If both high and low are won by a player or players who have no interest in the side money, then the side money is returned to the players who have bet it, irrespective of the relative rank of their hands.

(b) If a player who has no interest in the side money divides the pot with a player who has interest in the side money, the player with interest takes all the side money up to the extent of his interest therein.

Example: At the start of the hand A, B, C and D contest the pot. A has one hundred chips; B, two hundred; C and D, two hundred and fifty each. All the chips are bet so that at the conclusion of the hand the pot is four hundred chips, representing one hundred from each player; and the initial side money is three hundred chips, representing one hundred each from B, C and D; and there is a supplementary side-money pot of one hundred chips, representing fifty each from C and D. Should A win both high and low, all the side money goes back, irrespective of the relative rank of B, C and D. Should A win high and B win low, A and B divide the pot and B takes all the first side money, and C and D get their fifty chips back. Should A win high and C low, they divide the pot and C takes all the side money.

(c) In case a player with interest in the side money wins one way, and another player with interest in the side money ties for the other way with a player with no interest in the side money, two thirds of the side money goes to the player who takes one half of the main pot and one third to the player who gets one fourth of the main pot.

Going back to our previous example, let us assume C wins high and A and D tie for low: The four hundred chips in the main pot are divided two hundred to C, one hundred each to A and D. The four hundred chips in the two piles of side money are divided two thirds to C and one third to D.

(d) In case a player who has interest in the side money ties for one way, whereas no other player with interest in the side money wins the other way, he wins one half of the side money put up by the other players.

To go back to our previous example, suppose A wins high and ties for low with C. A takes three fourths of the main pot and C one fourth. B and D now each withdraw one half of their side money and C gets the rest.

Ace Low

By agreement the players may allow the ace to count as both an ace and a one. This has the effect of making the six, four, three, two, one the lowest hand.

In High-Low Seven-Card Stud, if a player has a full house the best low hand he can make includes a pair. Thus, if a man holds three deuces, two tens, a four and a five, his best low hand consists of two deuces, a ten, a four and a five. This produces several complicated situations. For instance, Player A has a king full on deuces and two odd cards; Player B has a three full on fours and two odd cards. Player A wins high with the king full and now wins low with a pair of deuces.

Or, going one step further, if the ace counts both high and low and Player A holds an ace full on threes and Player B a deuce full on kings, Player A wins high with his ace full and then, by counting his aces low, proceeds to win low also.

Declaring High-Low

There is a variation of High-Low Poker in which before the showdown each player declares whether he is trying to win high, low or both. The declaration is made according to one of the following methods:

Method A: The last player to bet or raise announces first, whereupon the other players, starting at his left, make their announcement.

Method B: A player places a white chip in his hand if he is going for low, a red chip if he is going for high and one of each color if he is going for both. The hands are then opened simultaneously.

The division of the pot in this game is based on the fact that a player may win only what he declares for and competes only with those players who declare the same way. Thus, if but one player declares low he automatically wins low, irrespective of the other hands. A player who declares both high and low wins nothing if he is beaten for high by any player who declares high, or for low by any player who declares low. In case no player wins what he declares for, the pot is divided.

Example: A, B and C are in the pot. A and B both declare high-low; C declares high. A has high; B has low. Neither A nor B can take the pot since they did not win what they declared for, while C cannot take the pot since A declared for high-low and beat him for high. Hence the pot is divided three ways.